TAKING The HEAT

Canadian Politicians in the Kitchen

Written & Compiled by
Yasmin John-Thorpe

Dedicated to politicians who are "taking the heat".

Published and copyrighted by Tobago International Inc.
Compiled by Yasmin John-Thorpe.
Cover photography and design by Stuart Bish Photography/Design, Penticton, British Columbia.
Book design and layout by Stuart Bish Photography/Design, Penticton, British Columbia.
Text editing by Alison Jacques. Some text edited for content and length.
Typesetting by Nancy Rasmussen.
Compiler's photo and photo of MLA Rick Thorpe courtesy of Penticton Western.
Photo of Cinnamon City chef courtesy of Aerro Photography.
Printed and bound in Canada by Friesens.

Tobago International Inc.
Casa Bella Vista
4011 Finnerty Road
Penticton, British Columbia
CANADA V2A 8W2

National Library of Canada Cataloguing in Publication Data

John-Thorpe, Yasmin, 1950 –
Taking the heat

Includes some text in French
ISBN 0-9688817-0-X

1. Cookery, Canadian. 2. Politicians–Canada–Miscellanea. I. Title.
TX715.6.J628 2001 641.5971 C2001-910526-6

The Contributors

Table of Contents

Table of Contents

Introduction

When I decided to compile a cookbook I had no idea how difficult a task I had set for myself. I am a writer, not a culinary expert, but my enjoyment in foods and their preparations would have eventually guided me to work on a cookbook. With the escalation of local millennium projects, the decision to compile a cookbook was brought forward and I searched for an unusual cookbook I would be interested in publishing.

I found the answer after an incident the media dubbed 'The brawl in the hall', which involved my husband, a British Columbia politician. My curiosity into the lives of Canadian politicians heightened after my husband took 'the heat' from the media and others over this incident in the Legislature.

I wondered if I could show Canadian politicians as ordinary people, doing something ordinary in their daily lives. The idea for "Taking The Heat: Canadian Politicians in the Kitchen" was born. I decided to ask Canadian elected and appointed officials to contribute their favourite recipes for a national cookbook. My request went out through faxes, e-mail and snail mail. Within hours I received several replies, while others took days, weeks, months and finally years. A project that began in October 1999, aimed at the millennium, turned into a labour of patience. I was at the mercy of an ever-changing political scene, but it was with a great deal of satisfaction that I watched the project grow and finally become a reality over two years. The contributor's recipes are reproduced as faithfully as possible, and appear in each section sorted alphabetically by province.

I have included a section called 'With Regret', at the end of the book, as I wanted to show I had contacted every politician across this great country, and also because some of the replies were priceless. I have included information on

Canadian wines because several recipes refer to wines, and Canadian wines are receiving world awards and medals for excellence.

My heartfelt thanks go to all those who took the time to respond to my request. This book is dedicated to you as the result of your thoughtfulness. Your generous contribution has other, more far reaching benefits, for as promised, all sale proceeds from the cookbook (after net costs) will be donated to food banks. I would also like to thank the City of Penticton Millennium Project, where the contribution of this cookbook is registered.

My gratitude is extended to Mr. John Bishop, Mr. Donald Ziraldo and Dr. Harry McWatters, who added their expertise to this book. Thanks to Stuart Bish for the fabulous cover design and layout, and to Nancy Rasmussen for the text input, and to Alison Jacques, who edited the text.

Also, to everyone who assisted in testing the recipes – the chefs at local restaurants, fellow members of Penticton Writers and Publishers and my wonderful friends – I could not have completed this interesting journey without your support and kindness.

Finally, my closing words are for all those who will try these recipes: "remember our politicians are just ordinary people we elect and from whom we demand extraordinary feats and perfection".

Enjoy,

Yasmin John-Thorpe
Co-founder, Penticton Writers and Publishers.
Co-Authored books:

- *"Penticton, British Columbia – A Silhouette of Four Seasons"*
- *"Supernatural British Columbia"*
- *"Penticton and Area Secrets & Surprises"*
- *"Lovescape: The Romantic Novella Magazines"*

Bishop's
BISHOP'S RESTAURANT LTD.
2183 West Fourth Avenue,
Vancouver, B.C. V6K 1N7
738-2025

Dear Yasmin,

What a concept, politicians deliberately putting themselves into the heat. In this case it s in their own home kitchens. Things will really begin to heat up all across the country with this unique collection of recipes by these well known Canadian cooks.

You ll find loads of good and interesting food to inspire you in these pages. Where else would you have such a taste of Canada.

So go ahead fire up your own stove and enjoy the heat of their delicious culinary creations.

You re in for a great adventure.

Best regards

John Bishop

Foreword

What a concept, politicians deliberately putting themselves into the heat. In this case it's in their own home kitchens.

Things will really begin to heat up all across the country with this unique collection of recipes by these well known Canadian cooks.

You'll find loads of good and interesting food to inspire you in these pages. Where else would you have such a taste of Canada?

So go ahead, fire up your own stove and enjoy the heat of their delicious culinary creations. You're in for a great adventure.

Best regards,

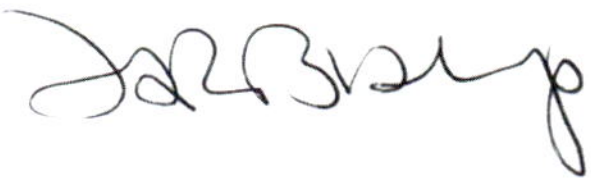

John Bishop
Owner and chef
Bishop's Restaurant
Vancouver, British Columbia

– Cookbooks by John Bishop:
"Bishop's: The Cookbook"
"Cooking at My House"

Senator Ross Fitzpatrick - page 65

Rich Coleman - page 15

Sindy Hawkins (with parents Sharan and Manohar Ahluwalia) page 51, 165

Taster Gordon Brown with chef Angelo Albano - page 19

Newfoundland Bakeapple berry - page 103

Peter Adams - page 143

Donald J. P. Ziraldo, Inniskillin - page 35, 166

Premier Paul Okalik (centre, back row) - page 83

Premier Gary Doer - page 73

Rick Thorpe and chef Mike Black - page 141, 165

SEAFOOD

Province of
British Columbia
Legislative Assembly

OFFICIAL OPPOSITION

R. T. (Rich) Coleman,
(Fort Langley-Aldergrove)

Constituency Office: 27118 Fraser Highway, Aldergrove, B.C. V4W 3P6
Telephone: (604) 857-9727 Fax: (604) 857-4983

Room 201, Parliament Buildings, Victoria, B.C. V8V 1X4
Telephone: (604) 387-2767 Fax: (604) 356-6176

BBQ Salmon

Ingredients:

Two salmon filets (skin on)
Montreal Steak Spice
Garlic salt
Curry powder
Seasoning salt
¼ lb. of butter
Ice cubes

Line a cookie sheet with tin foil and lay salmon filets on the sheet. Liberally sprinkle with steak spice, garlic salt and seasoning salt. Then sprinkle two pinches of curry powder over the fish. Let stand for an hour to allow some absorption of the spices into the raw fish.

Place on the barbecue at medium heat and put 6-8 ice cubes, together with half the butter, on top of the fish. Close the lid. When the first amount of butter has melted add the remainder. When both the ice cubes and the butter have melted, baste the fish with the liquid, and sprinkle the fish once more with the seasoning salt and the garlic salt.

Cooking time is from 15 to 20 minutes, depending on the thickness of the fish. As the fish cooks it's colour will change, from the outside edges, to a light greyish pink. When this colour spreads throughout the flesh it is ready.

Check the flesh at the thickest part with fork, as it is important not to overcook. Throughout the cooking process continue to baste with the liquid created. If you need more liquid add more ice cubes. The fish will pull off the skin with a fork when served hot to your guests.

Serve with:
Steamed onions – (wrap in tin foil with ice cubes and butter and place on the BBQ.)
Baked garlic
Assorted vegetables
Garlic bread
Salad

Quote:

"Without love, friendship and loyalty, one has nothing."

R.T. (Rich) Coleman, MLA
Official Opposition Whip

BBQ Salmon

Rich Coleman, MLA, Fort Langley–Aldergrove, British Columbia, Minister Public Safety and Solicitor General

2 salmon filets (skin on)
Montreal Steak spice
Garlic salt
Curry powder
Seasoning salt
1/4 pound butter
Ice cubes

Line a cookie sheet with tin foil, lay salmon filets on the sheet, sprinkle on steak spice, garlic salt and seasoning salt quite liberally. Sprinkle two pinches of curry over the fish. Let stand for an hour to allow some absorption of the spices into the raw fish.

Place on barbecue at medium heat, place 6-8 ice cubes and half the butter on top of the fish. Close the lid. When the first amount of butter has melted add the rest. When the ice cubes and butter have melted baste the fish with the liquid. Sprinkle the fish once more with the seasoning salt and the garlic salt.

Cooking time is from 15–20 minutes depending on the thickness of the fish. As the fish cooks its colour will change from the outside edges in to a light greyish pink. When the colour is throughout, the fish is ready. Check at the thicker part of the fish with a fork. Do not overcook. Throughout the cooking baste the fish with the liquid created; if you need more, add more ice cubes. Fish will pull off the skin with a fork when served hot to your guests.

Serve with steamed onions (onion wrapped in tin foil on BBQ with butter and an ice cube), baked garlic, assorted vegetables, garlic bread and salad.

"Simple to make and very tasty. I added whole crushed garlic cloves to butter in place of garlic salt. Served with steamed onions and tossed salad (romaine, watercress, sliced green olives, tomatoes, sliced hard boiled eggs, sliced cucumbers and feta cheese) in Balsamic vinaigrette."

– (Tester) Yasmin John-Thorpe, writer and cookbook compiler.

Notes:

"Without love, friendship and loyalty, one has nothing."

C. JEREMY DALTON, M.L.A.
WEST VANCOUVER-CAPILANO
PARILAMENT BUILDINGS
VICTORIA, B.C. V8V 1X4
TELEPHONE: (250) 356-3070

LEGISLATIVE ASSEMBLY
PROVINCE OF BRITISH COLUMBIA

CONSTITUENCY OFFICE:
SUITE 306, 1497 MARINE DRIVE
WEST VANCOUVER, B.C. V7T 1B8
TELEPHONE: (604) 925-1611
FACSIMILE: (604) 925-9658

"OYSTERS SUNSHINE COAST"
(FLIP COUNTRY!)

1. OBTAIN OYSTERS (PREFERABLY FREE --ie. FROM LASQUITI ISLAND, OR JEDIDIAH ISLAND AND MARINE PARK, OR JUDITH REID);

2. OPEN SAID OYSTERS REMOVING THE TOP SHELL;

3. PLACE HALF OYSTER ON THE BAR-BEE WITH SAUCE THEREIN (SOYA SAUCE, TABASCO, LEMON JUICE IF DESIRED AND APPROPRIATE SPICES);

4. BAKE UNTIL FIRM (NOT <u>TOO</u> FIRM);

5. EAT CONTENTS (NOT THE SHELL, WHICH IS ***HOT***!!) BEER OF COURSE IS A GREAT CHASER (OR VQA);

6. REPEAT 1 THROUGH 5 ABOVE.

7. WATCH YOUR LIBIDO!!!

8. WERE ***YOU*** IN WASHINGTON D.C. AUGUST 28, 1963? FLIP WAS.

Jeremy Dalton

JEREMY DALTON
from sunny Ambleside

Oysters Sunshine Coast

Jeremy Dalton, Former MLA, West Vancouver-Capilano, British Columbia

Open said oysters, removing the top shell.

Place half oyster on the bar-bee with sauce therein (soya sauce, Tabasco, lemon juice if desired and appropriate spices). Bake until firm (Not too firm).

Eat contents (Not the shell, which is **HOT!!**).

Repeat 1 through 5 above. Watch your libido!!!

Notes:

"I USED SHUCKED OYSTERS AND PLACED THEM ON SEA SHELLS. I ADDED LEMON JUICE, MELTED BUTTER AND VARIED FLAVOURS LIKE CRUSHED GARLIC CLOVES OR CRUSHED GINGER JUICE OR SOYA SAUCE TO GROUPS OF THE OYSTERS. TAKES ABOUT 10 – 15 MINUTES IN A CLOSED BARBECUE. MAKES A GREAT PLATTER OF APPETIZERS."

– (TESTER) YASMIN JOHN-THORPE, WRITER AND COOKBOOK COMPILER.

"Obtain oysters (preferably free – i.e., from Lasquiti Island, or Jedediah Island Marine Park, or Judith Reid)!"

LEGISLATIVE OFFICE:
RM. 201, PARLIAMENT BUILDINGS
VICTORIA, B.C. V8V 1X4
TELEPHONE: (250) 387-2805
FAX: (250) 387-8596

LEGISLATIVE ASSEMBLY
PROVINCE OF BRITISH COLUMBIA

CONSTITUENCY OFFICE:
3431 CHATHAM STREET
RICHMOND, B.C. V7E 2Y9
TELEPHONE: (604) 241-5590
FAX: (604) 241-4325

Geoff Plant, MLA (Richmond-Steveston)
OFFICIAL OPPOSITION OF BRITISH COLUMBIA

Manhattan Style Clam Chowder

FOR A LARGE CROWD…I prepared this recipe for the 1998 Steveston Salmon Festival Chowder Contest. My team, the Blazin' Ladles, won first place in the amateur division.

2½ lbs fresh clam meat, chopped
4 cloves fresh garlic, finely chopped
2 medium sweet yellow onions, finely chopped
4 medium Russet potatoes, peeled and diced
1 each red, green and yellow bell pepper, seeded and diced
4 celery stalks, finely chopped
3 carrots, finely chopped
2 Tbsp. Extra virgin olive oil
1 small ham hock
1 Tbsp. Tabasco sauce (hot so optional)
1 heaping tsp. oregano flakes
¼ bunch Italian parsley, finely chopped
2 cups rich red wine (Zinfandel or Merlot)
3 cups clam juice
2 quarts Clamato juice
1 16 ounce can tomato and green chili
1 8 ounce jar Spicy Red Pepper Pasta Sauce
1 16 ounce can Italian style diced tomato with basil
salt and pepper to taste

In a large pot (8 quart stock pot) bring Clamato juice, Clam juice, red wine, Tabasco sauce, ham hock, pasta sauce, tomatoes and green chili, and Italian tomato with basil to a boil. Reduce heat to a simmer.

In a large skillet heat olive oil, add onion, garlic and celery. Saute until translucent, add bell peppers and stir in oregano. To this add potatoes and carrots, stirring continuously for 2 minutes. Add skillet ingredients to the stock pot. Simmer for 1 ½ hours. Add fresh Clam meat and stir, cooking for a further 4 minutes. Add salt and pepper to taste. Serve, top with parsley.

Enjoy!

Geoff Plant, MLA
Richmond-Steveston

Manhattan Style Clam Chowder

Geoff Plant, MLA, Richmond–Steveston, British Columbia, Attorney General & Minister Responsible for Treaty Negotiations

2 1/2 pounds fresh clam meat, chopped
4 cloves fresh garlic, finely chopped
2 medium sweet yellow onions, finely chopped
4 medium Russet potatoes, peeled and diced
1 red, green and yellow bell pepper, seeded and diced
4 celery stalks, finely chopped
2 tablespoons extra virgin olive oil
1 small ham hock
1 tablespoon Tabasco sauce (hot, so optional)
1 heaping teaspoon oregano flakes
1/4 bunch Italian parsley, finely chopped
2 cups rich red wine (Zinfandel or Merlot)
3 cups clam juice
2 quarts Clamato juice
1 16–ounce can tomato and green chili
1 8–ounce jar Spicy Red Pepper pasta sauce
1 16–ounce can Italian–style diced tomato with basil
Salt and pepper to taste

In a large pot (8–quart stock pot) bring Clamato juice, clam juice, red wine, Tabasco sauce, ham hock, pasta sauce, tomatoes, green chili and Italian tomato with basil to a boil. Reduce heat to a simmer.

In a large skillet heat olive oil, add onion, garlic and celery. Sauté until translucent, add bell peppers and stir in oregano. To this add potatoes and carrots, stirring continuously for 2 minutes. Add skillet ingredients to the stock pot. Simmer for 1 1/2 hours. Add fresh clam meat and stir, cooking for a further 4 minutes. Add salt and pepper to taste. Serve, top with parsley.

"Easy to prepare. Lots of clams."

– (Tester) Angelo Albano, owner and chef Cinnamon City.

"This is very tasty. Lots of clams and wine gave it a nice flavour."

– (Taster) Gordon Brown, operations manager Overwaitea Foods.

Notes:

"This is for a large crowd. I prepared this recipe for the 1998 Steveston Salmon Festival Chowder Contest. My team, the Blazin' Ladles, won first place in the amateur division."

Official Opposition
Room 201, Parliament Buildings
Victoria, B.C. V8V 1X4
Phone: (250) 356-5200
Fax: (250) 387-8596

Constituency Office
101 – 191 Jensen Avenue East
PO Box 1356
Parksville, B.C. V9P 2H3
Phone: (250) 248-2604
Fax: (250) 248-7361

Province of
British Columbia
Legislative Assembly

Judith Reid, M.L.A.
(Parksville-Qualicum)

Oysters Rock-yer-Fella

1 dozen fresh British Columbia oysters
¼ cup of white wine
1 package Hollandaise sauce
1 package frozen chopped spinach
Bread crumbs
Butter
Parmesan cheese

1. Shuck the oysters and put in a bowl. Keep the deep-cupped half of the shell. Scrub the shells and set aside.
2. Add the wine to 2 cups water and bring to a boil.
3. Poach the oysters in the wine until water comes back to a boil and boil one more minute. Drain.
4. Prepare Hollandaise sauce according to package directions.
5. Defrost spinach in the microwave and then thoroughly squeeze out all liquid.
6. Add 1/3 of the Hollandaise sauce to the spinach. Use less spinach if desired.
7. Put a spoonful of spinach mixture in each oyster shell. Add an oyster and top it with a spoonful of Hollandaise sauce.
8. Mix bread crumbs with melted butter and parmesan cheese.
9. Top each oyster with a spoonful of bread crumbs.
10. Bake at 350 for 10 minutes or until crumbs are browned.

Judith Reid

Judith Reid, MLA
Parksville-Qualicum

Oysters Rock-yer-Fella

Judith Reid, MLA, Parksville–Qualicum, British Columbia, Minister of Transportation

1 dozen fresh British Columbia oysters
1/4 cup white wine
1 package hollandaise sauce
1 package frozen chopped spinach
Bread crumbs
Butter
Parmesan cheese

Shuck the oysters and put in a bowl. Keep the deep-cupped half of the shell. Scrub the shells and set aside.

Add the wine to 2 cups water and bring to a boil. Poach the oysters in the wine until water comes back to a boil and boil for one more minute. Drain.

Prepare hollandaise sauce according to package directions.

Defrost spinach in the microwave and then thoroughly squeeze out all liquid. Add 1/3 of the hollandaise sauce to the spinach. Use less spinach if desired. Put a spoonful of spinach mixture in each oyster shell. Add an oyster and top it with a spoonful of hollandaise sauce. Mix bread crumbs with melted butter and parmesan cheese. Top each oyster with a spoonful of bread crumbs.

Bake at 350°F for 10 minutes or until crumbs are browned.

"Tested these on five professional men who came to dinner. So tasty, they asked for seconds. I used pre-shucked oysters and one can of whole leaf spinach (drained and chopped) in place of frozen chopped spinach. May I suggest you replace package of hollandaise with the 'Blender Hollandaise' from the asparagus recipe on page 164."

– (Tester) Yasmin John-Thorpe, writer and cookbook compiler.

Notes:

Minister of the Environment | Ministre de l'Environnement

Ottawa, Canada K1A 0H3

Ottawa, October 20, 2000

Ms. Yasmin John-Thorpe
150 Adamson Court
Penticton, British Columbia
V2A 7R8

Dear Ms. John-Thorpe:

First, let me start by apologizing for the delay in responding to your request of August 15. Summer went very quickly but was also very busy.

I am pleased to provide you with a family recipe that has been in the Anderson's family for generation. I can also confirm to you today that I have cooked it myself several times!

Fish poached in Court Bouillon:

Ingredients:

- One large fish, plus fish parts
- Three cups of vegetable stock
- One cup of white wine
- Two tbs. salt
- One large onion chopped
- One medium whole onion with five cloves stuck in it
- Three carrots chopped

- One bay leaf
- Three sprigs of parsley
- Half tsp. thyme
- Three chopped stalks of celery
- Twelve bruised peppercorns

First: Put all the ingredients except the fish and the peppercorns into a fish poacher and boil for thirty minutes. This creates the "court bouillon".

.../2

- 2 –

Second: Wrap the fish with its skin on in cheesecloth so that both ends fall over the end of the poacher to provide a grip for lifting.

Third: When the bouillon is ready and still boiling hard lower the fish into the poacher and reduce heat to simmer. You should allow six to eight minutes per pound. Throw in the peppercorns. Make sure the liquid covers the fish. When the fish is opaque and ready to flake it is ready. Carefully lift it out, unwrap it and remove the skin. The fish will be delicious hot or cold.

I hope you will enjoy the recipe as much as my family does. Let me wish you good luck with your cooking!

Yours sincerely,

David Anderson

David Anderson, P.C., M.P.

Fish Poached in Court Bouillon

David Anderson, MP, Victoria, British Columbia, Minister of the Environment

1 large fish, plus fish parts
3 cups vegetable stock
1 cup white wine
2 tablespoons salt
1 chopped large onion
1 whole medium onion with five cloves stuck in
3 chopped carrots
1 bay leaf
3 sprigs parsley
1/2 teaspoon thyme
3 chopped stalks celery
12 bruised peppercorns

Notes:

Put all the ingredients except the fish and the peppercorns into a fish poacher and boil for 30 minutes. This creates the "court bouillon".

Wrap the fish with its skin on in cheesecloth so that both ends fall over the end of the poacher to provide a grip for lifting.

When the bouillon is ready and still boiling hard, lower the fish into the poacher and reduce heat to simmer. You should allow 6–8 minutes per pound. Throw in the peppercorns. Make sure the liquid covers the fish. When the fish is opaque and ready to flake it is ready. Carefully lift it out, unwrap it and remove the skin. This fish will be delicious hot or cold.

"A WONDERFUL ALTERNATIVE TO THE 'USUAL' FRIED FISH. I ENJOYED THIS UNION OF FLAVOURS WITH STEAMED BASMATI RICE FOR DINNER. AND COLD WITH A FRESH GREEN SALAD FOR LUNCH."

– (TESTER) SUE PREMACK, MEDICAL OFFICE ASSISTANT.

"I am pleased to provide you with a family recipe that has been in the Anderson family for generations. I can also confirm to you today that I have cooked it myself several times!"

GOVERNMENT OF
NEWFOUNDLAND AND LABRADOR

Department of Education

Office of the Minister

March 29, 2001

Yasmin John-Thorpe
Casa Bella Vista
4011 Finnerty Road
Penticton, BC
V2A 8W2

Dear Ms. John-Thorpe:

Thank you for inviting me to submit a recipe to your book *Taking the Heat: Canadian Politicians in the Kitchen*. Your title is an appropriate one. I'm sure many of my colleagues, like myself, like to cook and wish they had more time to do it.

I sent you a recipe for steamed mussels because mussels are a local seafood that play a large part of the diet of many Newfoundlanders and Labradorians. It is also a personal favorite of mine and I'm sure your readers will enjoy it.

Congratulations on your cookbook and best wishes for continued success.

Sincerely,

Judy M. Foote, MHA
District of Grand Bank
Minister of Education

P.O. Box 8700, West Block, Confederation Building, St. John's, Newfoundland, Canada, A1B 4J6,
Telephone (709) 729-5040, Facsimile (709) 729-0414

Steamed Mussels

Judy Foote, MHA, Grand Bank, Newfoundland and Labrador, Minister of Education

4–5 pounds fresh mussels, rinsed and clean of seaweed, etc. (Be sure to discard any mussels that remain open after you have tapped on their shells.)
1 1/2 cups red or white wine, beer or tomato juice (V8 or Clamato good too)
2 tablespoons olive oil
Splash of balsamic vinegar (about a tablespoon)
4–6 plum (Roma) tomatoes, diced small (or 3–4 field tomatoes)
1 red onion, diced
4 cloves garlic, minced
2 bay leaves
Fresh herbs of choice, minced (use 1/4 cup parsley, basil or cilantro, or 2 tablespoons oregano or thyme) OR 2 teaspoons dried herbs of choice (a nice combination is 1 1/2 teaspoon basil and 1/2 teaspoon thyme)
1 teaspoon each salt and freshly ground black pepper (or to taste)
Additional fresh herbs, chopped, to garnish, if desired
(An alternative to tomatoes and alcohol would be a tin of diced tomatoes with juice)

Heat oil in large pot on medium heat and sauté onion a few minutes until translucent. Add bay leaves and garlic, sauté a minute. (Don't let garlic burn – it gets bitter!) Add tomatoes, salt, pepper, sauté a minute. Turn heat to high and add wine, beer or juice, balsamic vinegar and herbs. Stir to combine and toss in mussels. Add just enough water to come one-third the way up to the top of the mussels. Cover and steam about 10 minutes until shells are open and mussels are cooked and plump. (Don't overcook!) Stir the pot a couple of times during cooking to ensure the flavours are well distributed and all mussels come in contact with cooking liquid. If pot threatens to boil over, adjust lid so a little steam can escape.

Ladle into bowls making sure each guest gets some of the liquid. Serves 4 people as a main course (with salad and lots of crusty bread for sopping up the stock) or 8-10 as an appetizer.

Leftover liquid makes great fish stock for red chowder or bouillabaisse!

"An easy recipe to make. Delicious."
– (Tester) Pamela Abbott, federal civil servant.

"So many people have busy lifestyles these days but we all love great food. Living close to the sea affords Newfoundlanders and Labradorians the luxury of fresh seafood. This recipe is quick, easy and flexible enough that you can use the vegetables and herbs that you have on hand. It's wonderful for entertaining or the quantities can be scaled down for an impromptu Friday night meal for two. As Minister of Education, I'm especially pleased to include a seafood recipe – seafood is brain food!"

Scallops Mornay

Jim Walsh

1/2 lb scallops
3/4 cup water
1/2 cup dry white wine
1/4 tsp salt
Dash white pepper
1/2 cup sliced fresh mushrooms
2 tbsp. chopped onion
1 tbsp. butter
4 tsp. flour
1/3 cup milk
1/4 cup shredded Swiss cheese
2 tbsp snipped Parsley (optional)
Hot cooked rice

In saucepan combine water, wine, salt
and pepper. bring to boil, add scallops
and mushrooms. return to boiling. Cover
and simmer 1 min. Remove scallops AND
mushrooms. set aside. Boil the liquid,
uncovered, for 10 min. till reduced to 1/2 cup

In another saucepan. cook onion in butter
until tender; stir in flour. Add the 1/2 cup
scallop liquid & milk. Cook & stir until
thickened, Stir in cheese until melted
Season with more salt & pepper if desired. Stir
in scallops & mushrooms Turn into two
10 oz. casseroles & Bake uncovered in 375°

for 15 to 20 minutes. Sprinkle
with Parsley Serve with hot cooked
rice. if desired.
Makes 2 servings

Media Quote

" To be enjoyed on the
first night as the government

Jim Walsh

Scallops Mornay

Jim Walsh, MHA, Conception Bay East and Bell Island, Newfoundland and Labrador, Parliamentary Secretary to the Minister of Municipal and Provincial Affairs for Housing

1/2 pound scallops
1/2 cup dry white wine
Dash white pepper
2 tablespoons chopped onions
4 teaspoons flour
1/4 cup shredded swiss cheese
Hot cooked rice (optional)
3/4 cup water
1/4 teaspoon salt
1/2 cup sliced fresh mushrooms
1 tablespoon butter
1/3 cup milk
2 tablespoons snipped parsley

Notes:

In saucepan combine water, wine, salt and pepper, bring to a boil. Add scallops and mushrooms, bringing back to a boil. Cover and simmer 1 minute. Remove scallops and mushrooms and set aside. Boil liquid uncovered for 10 minutes until liquid is reduced to 1/2 cup.

In another saucepan cook onion in butter until tender. Stir in flour. Add the 1/2 cup scallop liquid and milk. Cook, stirring until thickened. Stir in cheese until melted. Season with additional salt and pepper if desired. Stir in scallops and mushrooms. Turn into two 10-ounce casseroles and bake uncovered at 375°F for 10-15 minutes. Sprinkle with parsley. Serve with hot cooked rice, if desired. Makes 2 servings. Enjoy!

"A CREAMY, DELICIOUS TASTE OF THE SEA, WHICH CAN BE ENJOYED AS LUNCH OR DINNER ENTRÉE IN SMALLER PORTIONS OR AS A MAIN COURSE WITH A LEAFY GREEN SALAD."

- (TESTER) SUE PREMACK, MEDICAL OFFICE ASSISTANT.

"To be enjoyed on the first night of government."

Northwest Territories Chief of Staff

JUN 2 9 2000

Yasmin John-Thorpe
150 ADAMSON COURT
PENTICTON BC V2A 7R8

Dear Ms. John-Thorpe:

Taking The Heat: Canadian Politicians in the Kitchen

Please find attached Premier Kakfwi's recipe for Dene Calamari; a quote and a picture of the Premier, for the above mentioned cookbook.

Dene Calamari

Remove stomach and large intestine from fish by cutting out appropriate section.
Slice open along entire section and scrape clean.
Add garlic powder and grill over open fire for 5 – 7 minutes.
Eat while hot.

"Far From The Twisted Reach Of Crazy Sorrow" Bob Dylan

Sincerely,

Lynda Sorensen

Lynda Sorensen

Attachment

Government of the Northwest Territories, Yellowknife, NT Canada X1A 2L9 Fax: (867) 873-0385

Dene Calamari

Stephen Kakfwi, MLA, Sahtu Region, Premier of North West Territories

Remove stomach and large intestine from fish by cutting out appropriate section. Slice fish open along entire section and scrape clean. Add garlic powder and grill over open fire for 5-7 minutes. Eat while hot.

COMPILER'S NOTES: THIS IS A STRAIGHTFORWARD RECIPE FOR THE AVID FISHERMAN AND CAMPER. NO TESTING REQUIRED. ANY WHITE FISH WILL SUFFICE. PREMIER KAKFWI'S OFFICE SUGGESTS THE PREMIER IS PULLING MY "TENTACLE" BY CALLING THIS RECIPE DENE CALAMARI, SINCE THERE IS NO SQUID TO BE FOUND IN THE WATERS OFF THE NORTH WEST TERRITORIES. SO THERE IS NO DISAPPOINTMENT, I HAVE ASKED MARY THEODOSAKIS OF THEO'S GREEK RESTAURANT (FAMOUS FOR THEIR KALAMARI) TO SUBMIT A RECIPE. HERE IT IS

2 pounds Kalamari

Pull head away from body, discard the innards and quill bone. Cut out the eyes and small round cartilage at the base of tentacles. Rinse body and head under cool running water. Place Kalamari in bowl, add 1 tablespoon baking soda (used to tenderize-will not alter taste), add cold water to cover and refrigerate 1 hour. Rinse Kalamari thoroughly to remove baking powder and cut in 1″ rings, drain and pat dry. Place Kalamari in glass bowl and add:

1 tbsp. fresh crushed garlic
1 tbsp. crushed dry oregano
1 tsp. salt
1 tsp. black pepper
3 ounces white wine
3 ounces vegetable oil

Mix thoroughly, cover and refrigerate 1–2 hours or even better, overnight.

When ready to cook, place about 1 cup white flour and 1 tsp. salt in a plastic bag. Remove Kalamari from marinade and place in bag, dredge completely with flour. In heavy skillet, deep fryer or saucepan, heat vegetable oil (2–3″ deep) until very hot. Using kitchen tongs remove Kalamari, shaking off excess flour and add to hot oil. Fry quickly (2–3 minutes) until they are sandy coloured. Place on absorbent paper. Serve hot (topped with chopped parsley, finely diced onions, tomato wedges and a squeeze of fresh lemon) and with Tsatsiki dip or your favourite sauce.

"Close your eyes. You are sitting by the seaside with wonderful friends and family. The warm air and aroma of the sea surround you. Take a bite — enjoy!"

–WITH LOVE, MARY THEODOSAKIS, LOVER OF FOOD.

"Far From the Twisted Reach of Crazy Sorrow".
– Bob Dylan

House of Assembly
Nova Scotia

November 1, 1999

Ms. Yasmin John-Thorpe
150 Adamson Court
Penticton, BC V2A 7R8

Dear Madam:

Enclosed you will find a copy of one of my favorite recipes, a small photo as requested and a quote, which you can read below.

Having the sea for a neighbour and all the delicacies it provides to us, I feel it only appropriate to share one simple and yet "all occasion" recipe, fit for the most formal feast as well as for a very casual luncheon.

I hope you and your readers will enjoy it as much as we do here in Chester-St. Margaret's.
As for a quote, how about the following:
"*You never know when a good deed comes home to rest*".

Wishing you the best of success in your publication.

Sincerely,

John Chataway
MLA, Chester-St. Margaret's

Printed on paper that contains recycled fibre

Seafood Chowder

John Chataway, MLA, Chester–St. Margaret's, Nova Scotia

Peel and dice 4 medium potatoes.

Peel and dice 1 small to medium onion.

Put in 3-quart heavy bottom sauce pan with enough water to cover.

Add 1/2 teaspoon salt.

Simmer approximately 10 minutes until potatoes begin to lose transparency.

Lay one pound of haddock fillet over potatoes and add 2 bay leaves.

Cover and simmer an additional 10 minutes until fish begins to flake.

Add 1 pound of scallops and one tin of frozen lobster thawed.

Continue to simmer until all fish is cooked.

Add 1 large finely grated carrot, 1 can of Carnation milk and 1 pint of fresh whole milk.

Remove bay leaves.

Heat to just under boil; watch and stir.

When hot, add 1 cup of grated cheddar cheese; stir until cheese is melted.

Then add 2 tablespoons of butter and salt and pepper to taste.

Ladle into serving bowls; garnish with fresh parsley and chives.

Serve with rolls and/or crackers.

Approximate cooking time: 30 minutes

Serves 4 people as a main course, 8 people as an appetizer.

Note: This recipe can be prepared to the "add milk" stage, and then reheated and milk added just before serving.

"This is a very easy recipe to follow. I substituted fresh lobster tail and fresh cod for canned lobster and haddock fillet. The scallops added the most taste to this very rich dish, so I would recommend you serve in small portions as a soup starter. Our customers commented on the wonderful taste of this chowder."

– (Tester) Lance Thompson, owner/chef Cubby Hole Restaurant

Notes:

"You never know when a good deed comes home to rest."

PO Box 698
Halifax, Nova Scotia
B3J 2T9

Bus 902 424-4037
Fax 902 424-0594

Our File Number:

Department of Natural Resources
Office of the Minister

Nova Scotia

October 19, 1999

Mrs. Yasmin John-Thorpe
150 Adamson Court
Penticton, BC V2A 7R8

Dear Mrs. John-Thorpe:

Thank you for your recent letter outlining your project to compile a cookbook for the new millennium. I am pleased to contribute one of my favourite recipes which I hope your readers will enjoy as much as I do.

Since my appointment to the Cabinet is very recent, any off-base media quotes are fairly limited; however, I am sure there will be some along the way.

Best wishes for a successful venture.

Yours sincerely,

Ernest L. Fage
Minister

Enclosures

Printed on paper that contains recycled fibre

Lobster & Scrambled Eggs

Ernest L. Fage, MLA, Cumberland North, Nova Scotia, Minister Natural Resources, Agriculture and Fisheries

1/4 cup chopped celery
1 chopped medium onion

In a large skillet, sauté chopped celery and chopped onion in bacon drippings until tender.

1 large can cold pack lobster (knuckles and claws)
6 eggs
1/4 cup milk
Salt and pepper

Drain the can of cold pack lobster (knuckles and claws). Cut up the larger pieces and add to the sauteed vegetables. Heat through. Beat together eggs, milk, salt and pepper. Scramble egg mixture into lobster and vegetables. Serve hot, with fresh biscuits and strawberries.

Cloud Biscuits

Mix together:
4 cups flour
4 teaspoons cream of tartar
2 teaspoons baking soda
1 tablespoon white sugar
1 teaspoon salt

Cut in 1 cup shortening. Mix in 1 1/3 cups milk and 2 beaten eggs. Knead lightly on floured board and cut with biscuit cutter. Bake for 10 minutes at 400˚F.

Top with strawberries (fresh or frozen), sliced, with a teaspoon of sugar on them.

"Canned lobster very pricey. I substituted Atlantic lobster–flavoured Alaskan Char. The ladies at the birthday luncheon loved it. Biscuits were perfect complement to dish."

– (Tester) Yasmin John-Thorpe, writer and cookbook compiler.

Notes:

"Since my appointment to the Cabinet is very recent, any off-base media quotes are fairly limited; however, I am sure there will be some along the way."

Inniskillin

VQA

Fennel Scented Pickerel with Fiddleheads and Double Smoked Bacon Sauce

Serves 4.

1 pickerel, 3 lb. or 1.5 kg, cleaned and cut into 4 portions (medallions)
2 tbsp. olive oil
1 tbsp. fennel seeds, crushed
1 tsp. sea salt
1 tsp. peppercorns, crushed
1/2 Vidalia or other sweet onion, finely sliced
1/2 fennel, finely sliced
1/2 red pepper, finely sliced
1 tbsp. butter
1 cup fiddleheads, cleaned and blanched.
1 cup double smoked bacon sauce
salt, pepper

Rub pickerel medallions with olive oil, followed by mixture of fennel seeds, salt, peppercorns. Marinate 4 hours or overnight. Sweat onion, fennel, red peppers in butter. Add fiddleheads, sauté for another 1 minute or 2 (do not overcook or fiddleheads will fall apart). Add bacon sauce, keep warm while preparing fish. Sear pickerel in a tablespoon of olive oil over high heat. Finish in oven preheated to 400°F for 3-4 minutes. Serve with vegetable mixture and sauce.

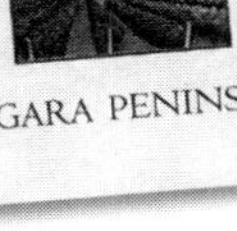

VQA NIAGARA PENINSULA VQA

Fennel Scented Pickerel with Fiddleheads and Double Smoked Bacon Sauce

Donald J.P. Ziraldo, President, Inniskillin and Okanagan Vineyards

1 pickerel, 3 pounds or 1.5 kg, cleaned and cut into 4 portions (medallions)
2 tablespoons olive oil
1 tablespoon fennel seeds, crushed
1 teaspoon sea salt
1 teaspoon peppercorns, crushed
1/2 Vidalia or other sweet onion, finely sliced
1/2 fennel, finely sliced
1/2 red pepper, finely sliced
1 tablespoon butter
1 cup fiddleheads, cleaned and blanched
1 cup double smoked bacon sauce
Salt, pepper

Rub pickerel medallions with olive oil, followed by mixture of half of the fennel seeds, salt, peppercorns. Marinate 4 hours or overnight. Sweat onion, fennel, red peppers in butter. Add fiddleheads, sauté for another 1 minute or 2 (do not overcook or fiddleheads will fall apart). Add bacon sauce, keep warm while preparing fish. Sear pickerel in a tablespoon of olive oil over high heat. Finish in oven preheated to 400°F for 3-4 minutes. Serve with vegetable mixture and sauce. Serves 4.

Double Smoked Bacon Sauce

Makes 1 cup (250ml).

3 thick slices double smoked bacon, cut into lardins (1" or .5cm pieces)
1 teaspoon butter
1 garlic clove, minced
Sprig of fresh thyme
5 tablespoons Sherry
1/3 cup (100 ml) chicken stock
1 cup (250 ml) cream
Salt, pepper

Melt butter in a saucepan, add bacon, sauté until golden. Add garlic, thyme and sherry. Sauté for a few minutes, stirring. Add stock, reduce by half, add cream, lower heat and continue simmering for 10-15 minutes. Adjust seasoning and pass through sieve before serving.

"MADE THE DISH WITH COD (FRESH PICKEREL NOT AVAILABLE) AND SUBSTITUTED GREEN BEANS FOR FIDDLEHEADS (NOT IN SEASON). TURNED OUT GREAT. BACON SAUCE ADDS AN INTERESTING TWIST TO WHITE FISH."

– (TESTER) RALPH H. KORDASS C.C.C., HEAD CHEF MAGNUM'S ON THE LAKE RESTAURANT, LAKESIDE RESORT AND CASINO.

Notes:

GOVERNMENT HOUSE
CHARLOTTETOWN
PRINCE EDWARD ISLAND
C1A 7L9

March 24, 2000

Ms. Yasmin John-Thorpe
150 Adamson Court
Penticton, BC, V2A 7R8

Dear Ms. John-Thorpe:

This will acknowledge receipt of your fax of March 22, 2000, seeking recipes for your **Taking the Heat: Canadian Politicians in the Kitchen** cookbook.

Enclosed is a favourite of mine - The Governor's Casserole - which of course must be made with Prince Edward Island scallops to enhance the flavour!

I have also enclosed a photo as requested.

Good luck in your endeavours.

Sincerely,

Gilbert H Clements

Gilbert R. Clements
Lieutenant Governor of Prince Edward Island

/jab

encls.

The Governor's Casserole

Gilbert R. Clements, Former Lieutenant-Governor of Prince Edward Island

1 pound scallops
Salt
2 tablespoons butter
1/2 cup chopped onion
1 cup sliced mushrooms
1 cup chopped green pepper
1/2 cup chopped celery
1/4 cup butter
1/4 cup flour
1 teaspoon salt
2 cups milk
1-2 cups soft bread crumbs
1-2 tablespoons melted butter
1/4 cup finely grated cheddar cheese

Notes:

Separate scallops and sprinkle with salt.

Melt butter and pan fry mushrooms, green pepper, celery and onion. Stir for about 10 minutes until partly cooked but not limp. Make a medium white sauce by combining and cooking butter, flour and milk.

When thickened, add scallops and partly cooked vegetables. Combine thoroughly and place in a greased 1 1/2 quart casserole. Top with buttered crumbs to cover. Sprinkle cheese over crumbs.

Bake 20 minutes at 375°F or until bubbly around the edges and crumbs are delicately browned. Makes 6 servings.

"EASY TO FOLLOW AND SIMPLE TO PREPARE. I WOULDN'T CHANGE A THING."

– (TESTER) RALPH H. KORDASS C.C.C., HEAD CHEF MAGNUM'S ON THE LAKE RESTAURANT, LAKESIDE RESORT AND CASINO.

"...must be made with Prince Edward Island scallops to enhance the flavour!"

Prince Edward Island
CANADA

Tel 902 368 5120
Fax 902 368 5385
http://www.gov.pe.ca/

Transportation and Public Works

Office of the Minister
PO Box 2000
Charlottetown
Prince Edward Island
Canada C1A 7N8

November 8, 1999

Yasmin John-Thorpe
150 Adamson Court
Penticton BC V2A 7R8

Dear Ms. John-Thorpe:

Thank you for your E-mail dated October 4, 1999 in which you requested a recipe for your book "Taking the Heat: Canadian Politicians in the Kitchen."

As requested, enclosed is a recipe for Lobster Casserole as well a photograph and bio.

Good luck with your endeavor.

Sincerely,

Michael F. Currie
Minister

/sms

Encl:

Lobster Casserole

Michael F. Currie, MLA, Georgetown–Baldwin's Road, Prince Edward Island, Minister Development and Technology

1/2 cup butter, melted
1/2 cup flour
2 cups milk
1 tin lobster
1 tin chopped scallops (optional)
1 green pepper
1 cup mushrooms
1 cup bread crumbs
1 cup cheddar cheese
3 tablespoons white wine

Notes:

In a saucepan melt butter. Stir in flour and milk. Cook over low heat, stirring until thick. Add lobster and chopped scallops, green pepper and mushrooms. Season with salt, pepper and white wine. Place in a casserole dish. Sprinkle with bread crumbs, grated cheese and butter. Bake at 350°F for 1 1/2 hours.

"This is an easy recipe to follow. The combination gives a delicious taste."

– (Tester) Marilyn Peterson, small business owner/operator.

Cream of Crab Soup

Elinor Caplan, MP, Thornhill, Ontario, Minister of Citizenship and Immigration

1 10–ounce can condensed mushroom soup
1 10–ounce can condensed asparagus soup
1 5–ounce can crab meat (drained)
2 cups light cream
1/4 cup sherry

Mix all ingredients. Heat and serve. Serves 6–8.

"Very easy to make and very tasty. This is a great soup for those cool fall and winter nights."

– (Testers) Lewis Knee, astronomer, and Ana Maria Stiepovic, Spanish instructor.

MEAT & POULTRY

ED-000XXX

ALBERTA
MINISTER OF ECONOMIC DEVELOPMENT

August 28, 2000

Ms. Yasmin John-Thorpe
150 Adamson Court
Penticton, BC V2A 7R8

Ms. John-Thorpe

Thank you for your recent letter regarding the "Taking the Heat: Canadian Politicians in the Kitchen" cookbook in which you are compiling.

I appreciate the opportunity to participate in such a project. Enclosed is my photo, and a recipe of my famous "Havelock Hearty Stew."

If I can be of further assistance please contact my office at (780) 427-3162.

Yours truly,

Jon Havelock, Q.C.
Minister of Economic Development
MLA Calgary-Shaw

Enclosures

103 Legislature Building, Edmonton, Alberta, Canada T5K 2B6 Telephone 780/427-3162 Fax 780/422-6338

Printed on recycled paper

Havelock's Hearty Stew

Jon Havelock, Former MLA, Calgary-Shaw, Alberta, Former Minister of Economic Development

2 pounds stew meat (or round steak), cut in 1" cubes.

Dredge in flour and fry in small amount of oil until brown, drain off fat and add:

2 cups beef stock (use beef bouillon cubes)
4 carrots, chopped
4-5 potatoes, chopped
3 onions, quartered
1 stalk celery with tops, cut up
1 bay leaf
1 clove garlic, chopped
1 teaspoon Worchestershire sauce
1 tablespoon salt (a little less at first)
1/2 teaspoon pepper
1 teaspoon paprika

Stir all ingredients and bring to a gentle boil. Reduce heat and cook on low for 2-3 hours until meat is tender.

"Very tasty. The paprika gives a nice 'kick' to warm you on a chilly day. Try adding one can cream of mushroom soup. For thicker gravy, add 2 tbsp. cornstarch dissolved in 1/2 cup water. Can also be cooked in a slow cooker on high for 4 hours."

– (Tester) Janelle Breese-Biagioni, author.

Notes:

THE PREMIER OF ALBERTA

Ralph's Chili

2 tablespoons olive oil
1 1/2 cups chopped onions
8 large garlic cloves, minced
3 pounds ground beef
1 pound of uncased hot italian sausage (hot is great!)
5 tablespoons chili powder
1 tablespoon ground cumin
1 teaspoon dried basil
1/2 teaspoon dried oregano
1 28-ounce can crushed tomatoes
Hot sauce to taste
1 bottle of beer
1 6-ounce can tomato paste
1 14 ounce can of kidney beans
Remove the niblets of 3 ears of Taber corn – if you're not lucky enough to live in Alberta you can use one 14 ounce can of niblet corn

Heat oil in a large pot over medium-heat. Add onions and garlic. Sauté until onions translucent. Set aside onions and garlic. Brown meats, beef and sausage. Return onions and garlic. Add chili powder, cumin, basil, and oregano. Cook for 15 – 20 minutes. Drain any excess oils. Mix in tomatoes, beer, hot sauce and tomato paste. Mix in beans and corn Simmer about 3 hours or until it reaches desired consistency. Season to taste with salt and pepper…more hot sauce. (Can be prepared 3 days ahead. Refrigerate until cold, then cover. Re warm over low heat before serving.

Serves 8 to 10.

Legislature Building, Edmonton, Alberta, Canada T5K 2B6 Telephone (403) 427-2251 Fax (403) 427-1349

Ralph's Chili

Ralph Klein, MLA, Calgary Elbow, Premier of Alberta

2 tablespoons olive oil
1 1/2 cups chopped onions
8 large garlic cloves, minced
3 pounds ground beef
1 pound uncased hot Italian sausage (hot is great!)
5 tablespoons chili powder
1 tablespoon ground cumin
1 teaspoon dried basil
1/2 teaspoon dried oregano
1 28-ounce can crushed tomatoes
Hot sauce to taste
1 bottle of beer
1 6-ounce can tomato paste
1 14-ounce can kidney beans
Remove the niblets of 3 ears of Taber corn – if you're not lucky enough to live in Alberta you can use one 14–ounce can of niblet corn

Heat oil in a large pot over medium heat. Add onions and garlic. Sauté until onions are translucent. Set aside onions and garlic. Brown meats, beef and sausage. Return onions and garlic. Add chili powder, cumin, basil and oregano. Cook for 15–20 minutes. Drain any excess oils. Mix in tomatoes, beer, hot sauce and tomato paste. Mix in beans and corn. Simmer about 3 hours or until it reaches desired consistency. Season to taste with salt and pepper... more hot sauce. Refrigerate until cold, then cover. Re-warm over low heat before serving.

Serves 8–10.

"THE RECIPE WAS EASY TO FOLLOW AND ALSO QUITE SIMPLE TO PREPARE."

– (TESTER) RALPH H. KORDASS C.C.C., HEAD CHEF MAGNUM'S ON THE LAKE RESTAURANT, LAKESIDE RESORT AND CASINO.

Notes:

"Can be prepared 3 days ahead."

George Abbott, MLA, Shuswap
Province of British Columbia
Legislative Assembly

Constituency Address:
103, 320 Alexander Street NE. (Box 607)
Salmon Arm, British Columbia V1E 4N7
Phone: (250) 833-1815 Fax: (250) 832-1744

Room 109, Parliament Buildings
Victoria, British Columbia V8V 1X4
Phone: (250) 387-2549 Fax: (250) 387-2550

George Abbott, MLA, Shuswap

Dad's Meatloaf

1 lb. lean ground beef
1 egg
½ onion
1 C rolled oats
3 T ketchup
3 T relish
1 T mustard

Mix the whole mess together. Cook until chances of e-coli poisoning are extinguished.

G. M. Abbott

"Surly to bed, surly to rise ..."

George Abbott

Dad's Meatloaf

George Abbott, MLA, Shuswap, British Columbia, Minister of Community, Aboriginal and Women's Services

1 pound lean ground beef
1 egg
1/2 onion, chopped
1 cup rolled oats
3 tablespoons ketchup
3 tablespoons relish
1 tablespoon mustard

Notes:

Mix the whole mess together. Cook until chances of E.coli poisoning are extinguished.

"Cook for 45 mins. to 1 hour. Cool or it falls apart when sliced. I usually don't add all these condiments to my meatloaf, so I could definitely taste them."

- (Tester) Penny Smith, young-adult author.

"Surly to bed, surly to rise ..."

Bishop's

BISHOP'S RESTAURANT LTD.
2183 West Fourth Avenue,
Vancouver, B.C. V6K 1N7
738-2025

Braised Lamb Stew

This dish is complete with meat and vegetables, all cooked and served from one favourite casserole. It can be prepared with chicken, beef or pork

1 ¼ lb. boneless leg of lamb
1 cup flour
2 tbsp vegetable oil for frying
1 cup red wine
2 cups stock or water
salt and pepper

½ cup finely chopped onion
½ cup finely diced carrot
½ cup finely diced celery
2 chopped cloves garlic
2 tbsp tomato paste
1 tsp fennel seeds

Preheat oven to 375 F.

If you decide to buy a leg of lamb with the bone in and debone it yourself, keep any trim and bone to make the stock for this dish.
Cut meat into 2 – 3 inch cubes. Season with salt and pepper. Dip each cube into flour, coating all sides.
In a frying pan heat vegetable oil to medium. When hot, add lamb chunks and sauté until all sides are brown. Remove lamb and place in a casserole or baking dish. Return frying pan to the burner and add chopped vegetables, sauté for 5 minutes. Add tomato paste, red wine and fennel seeds. Stir well and pour over the lamb. Top the casserole with the water or stock. Cover with lid or seal with aluminum foil. Bake for 1½ hours.
Serve with Rosemary Dumplings.

Braised Lamb Stew with Rosemary Dumplings

John Bishop, Bishop's Restaurant, Vancouver, British Columbia

This dish is complete with meat and vegetables, all cooked and served from one favourite casserole. It can be prepared with chicken, beef or pork.

1 1/4 pound boneless leg of lamb
1 cup flour
2 tablespoons vegetable oil for frying
1 cup red wine
2 cups stock or water
Salt and pepper
1/2 cup finely chopped onion
1/2 cup finely diced carrot
1/2 cup finely diced celery
2 chopped cloves garlic
2 tablespoons tomato paste
1 teaspoon fennel seeds

Preheat oven to 375°F.

If you decide to buy a leg of lamb with the bone in and de-bone it yourself, keep any trim and bone to make the stock for this dish.

Cut meat into 2- to 3-inch cubes. Season with salt and pepper. Dip each cube into flour, coating all sides.

In a frying pan heat vegetable oil to medium. When hot, add lamb chunks and sauté until all sides are brown. Remove lamb and place in a casserole or baking dish. Return frying pan to the burner and add chopped vegetables, sauté 5 minutes. Add tomato paste, red wine and fennel seeds. Stir well and pour over the lamb. Top the casserole with the water or stock. Cover with lid or seal with aluminum foil. Bake for 1 1/2 hours. Serve with Rosemary Dumplings.

Rosemary Dumplings

1 cup flour
1 teaspoon baking powder
1/2 teaspoon salt
1 teaspoon chopped rosemary leaves
2 tablespoons olive oil
1/2 cup milk

Combine flour, baking powder, salt and rosemary in a bowl. Add the olive oil and milk. Mix together to form a soft dough. Divide the dough into six pieces.

Remove stew from oven. Taste and check seasoning. Add salt and pepper to taste. Place dumplings on top of the stew. Cover and bake for a further 15–20 minutes. The dumplings should be light and fluffy when they are ready.

"THIS IS AN EASY RECIPE TO FOLLOW AND IS MOUTH WATERING."

– (TESTER) YASMIN JOHN-THORPE, WRITER AND COOKBOOK COMPILER.

Province of
British Columbia
Legislative Assembly

Sindi Hawkins M.L.A.
(Okanagan West)

OFFICIAL OPPOSITION OF BRITISH COLUMBIA

Constituency Office: 102, 2121 Ethel Street, Kelowna, B.C. V1Y 2Z6
Telephone: (250) 717-1570 Fax: (250) 717-8300
Email: sindi@telus.net

Parliament Buildings, Victoria, B.C. V8V 1X4
Telephone: (250) 387-2725 Fax: (250) 387-2731

March 27, 2001

Yasmin Thorpe
4011 Finwerty Rd.
Penticton, BC
V2A 8W2

Dear Yasmin,

Thank you for asking for my favourite recipes. Here are two recipes that are considered 'comfort food' in my home. My four sisters and I grew up learning to cook at my mother's side. We would watch in awe as she chopped, mixed and dashed together various ingredients to create culinary masterpieces without using so much as a spoon or measuring cup! I hope these recipes do her justice. Enjoy!

Sincerely,

Sindi

Sindi

All The Best on your project ♥ S

Chicken Curry with Yoghurt

Sindi Hawkins, MLA, Okanagan–Mission, British Columbia, Minister Responsible for Health Planning

1/3 cup oil
4 large onions, finely chopped
6 cloves garlic, finely chopped
2 tablespoons finely grated fresh ginger
2 8-ounce cans crushed tomatoes
2 teaspoons ground coriander
1 cup chopped fresh sprigs coriander
fresh long green chilli peppers
6 pounds chicken, skinned and cut into pieces
2 cups water
2 teaspoons ground cumin
2 teaspoons tumeric
1 1/2 teaspoons salt
2 teaspoons paprika
1/2 teaspoon cayenne
2 teaspoons garam masala
1 cup yoghurt

Heat oil in large heavy pot on medium high heat. Add onion, garlic and ginger, frying until onion is golden. Add water, paprika, cumin, coriander and salt. Bring to a low boil. Add crushed tomatoes and 1 teaspoon garam masala, continuing to cook on low to medium heat until mixture is thick and lets oil. In a shallow pan lightly brown chicken pieces. Add to tomato mixture and continue cooking on medium to low heat until meat is well cooked, 45-60 minutes. (I like the meat to fall off the bones.) Drain off oil. Gently stir in yoghurt on low heat until heated thoroughly. Garnish with fresh coriander, fresh chilli peppers to taste and remainder of garam masala. Serve with Muttar Chawal (rice and peas) – see page 165.

"THIS IS A RED CURRY. THE SPICES CAN BE FOUND IN SPECIALTY SHOPS. THE RICH SMELLS FILL THE HOUSE. VERY, VERY TASTY. THE RICE (MUTTAR CHAWAL, PAGE 165) IS A GREAT ADDITION TO THE CURRY CHICKEN RECIPE."

– (TESTER) ROBERTA ROBERTSON, INTERIOR DECORATOR AND CHEF.

Notes:

"All the best on your project."

Gerard Janssen, MLA
(Alberni)
Parliament Buildings
Victoria, B.C. V8V 1X4
Phone: (604) 387-0967
Fax: (604) 356-0596

Community Office:
4859 Johnston Road
Port Alberni, B.C. V9Y 5M2
Phone: (604) 724-4454
Fax: (604) 724-9314

Province of British Columbia
Legislative Assembly

Gerard Janssen, MLA
(Alberni)

BAMI PANGHANG

(Dutch Indonesian Dish)

Chicken Breast or Lean Pork
4 tbsp cooking oil
3 Big Onions
3 Red Peppers (or green)

Cooked Rice or Noodles

5 tbsp Vinegar
5 tbsp Konimex Ketjab
(or sweet soya sauce)
1 cup Heinz Tomato Ketchup
1/2 tsp Sambal (Konimex)
1 tbsp Sugar (to taste)

---

1. Cut meat in small bite size pieces. Brown in 2 tbsp cooking oil and set aside.
2. In the same pan, add 2 more tablespoons of oil. Gently fry onions and peppers, stirring to keep from browning. You may add a can of drained mushrooms if you like. Add meat to onions and peppers. Keep warm.
3. In a separate bowl, mix together all remaining ingredients and add to meat mixture all at once. Bring to a boil, stirring constantly. Turn down heat, simmer for one hour.
4. If desired, thicken mix with cornstarch and serve over rice (or noodles if preferred).
5. Smakelisk Eeten!

Gerard Janssen, MLA
Alberni

Bami Panghang (Dutch Indonesian Dish)

Gerard Janssen, Former MLA, Alberni, British Columbia

Chicken breast or lean pork
4 tablespoons cooking oil
3 big onions, chopped
3 red peppers (or green), chopped
5 tablespoons vinegar
5 tablespoons Konimex Ketjab (or sweet soya sauce)
1 cup Heinz Tomato Ketchup
1/2 teaspoon Sambal (Konimex)
1 tablespoon sugar (to taste)
Cooked rice or noodles

Notes:

Cut meat in small bite-size pieces. Brown in 2 tablespoons cooking oil and set aside.

In the same pan, add 2 more tablespoons of oil. Gently fry onions and peppers, stirring to keep from browning. You may add a can of drained mushrooms if you like. Add meat to onions and peppers. Keep warm.

In a separate bowl, mix together all remaining ingredients and add to meat mixture all at once. Bring to a boil, stirring constantly. Turn down heat, simmer for 1 hour.

If desired, thicken mix with cornstarch and serve over rice (or noodles if preferred).

"A very tasty dish. Thai-tasting recipe."

- (Tester/Taster) Wendy Bosma, owner Gun Barrel Grill Restaurant.

"Smakelisk Eeten!"

SUMAC
RIDGE
ESTATE WINERY

Harry McWatters
President

May 22, 2001

Yasmin Thorpe
Casa Bella Vista
4011 Finnerty Road
Penticton, BC V2A 8W2

Dear Yasmin:

Congratulations Yasmin, on the successful completion of the cookbook. This was an enormous task and your efforts are to be commended.

Good luck, good cooking and bon appetite!

Cheers!!

Harry McWatters
President, Sumac Ridge Estate Wine Group
Founding Chairman, British Columbia Wine Institute
Founding Chairman, VQA Canada

RHM/st

D:\My Documents\Correspondence\0522-08.doc

SUMAC RIDGE ESTATE WINERY LTD.
17403 HIGHWAY 97, P.O.BOX 307
SUMMERLAND B.C. CANADA
V0H 1Z0
TEL.(604)494-0451 FAX(604)494-3456

Harry's Corn Chowder

Dr. Harry McWatters, Sumac Ridge Estate Winery, Summerland, British Columbia

6 slices bacon
5 potatoes, diced to 1/2" cubes
1 large onion, diced
2 10-ounce packages frozen corn (Peaches and Cream if possible)
1 cup water
3 cups light cream
1 tablespoon sugar
1/2 cup butter
2 teaspoons salt
1/4 teaspoon black pepper
1 dash cayenne

Notes:

Cook bacon (to crisp) in a large pan and remove from pan.

Sauté garlic and onion in bacon grease. Drain grease. Add water and potatoes, cook 10 minutes. Add remaining ingredients. Cook for 10 minutes over low heat.

Serve in bowls with bacon crumbled over the top.

Optional version: Clams may be added to above.

Freezes well-may be prepared ahead of time. Serves 8.

Best with VQA Chardonnay (oaked).

"EASY AND DELICIOUS. I SUBSTITUTED SKIM MILK, SO IT TURNED OUT A LITTLE THIN."

– (TESTER) MAUREEN MCDONALD, SPORTS ENTHUSIAST AND ADVENTURE TRAVELLER.

"Good luck, good cooking and bon appetite!"

Parliament Buildings
Victoria, B.C. V8V 1X4
Phone: (250) 387-2618
Fax: (250) 387-2731

Constituency Office
102, 2232 Marine Drive
West Vancouver, B.C. V7V 1K4
Phone: (604) 926-2815
Fax: (604) 981-0010
Toll Free: 1-800-414-8211
Email: ted.nebbeling.mla@leg.bc.ca
Internet: www.tednebbeling.com

Province of British Columbia
Legislative Assembly

OFFICIAL OPPOSITION OF BRITISH COLUMBIA

Ted Nebbeling, M.L.A.
(West Vancouver-Garibaldi)

TED NEBBELING'S FAVOURITE

1 lb. pork tenderloin, veal or chicken breast
6 oz. mushrooms
2 cloves garlic
2 teaspoons of capers and two teaspoons of caper juice
12 leaves of basil or 1 teaspoon of basil paste
4 pieces of sun dried tomatoes (soaked in hot water for ten minutes)
Half a cup of white wine
250 ml cream
Olive oil
1 tablespoon of butter
Salt and pepper to taste
Fettuccini for 4

Pre-Prep
Cut meat in small pieces, slice mushrooms, chop garlic, cut sun dried tomatoes in small pieces, salt and pepper meat and dust with flour

Now Let's Cook
- Cook fettuccini in rolling boiling water (do not overcook)
- Heat olive oil and butter in frying pan (make sure it is hot)
- Add meat and fry until brown and simmer for 3 minutes stirring occasionally
- Add sliced mushrooms and chopped garlic and simmer until most of the liquid has evaporated
- Add capers, juice, sun dried tomatoes and basil
- Stir and let cook on low heat for four minutes; bring heat back to maximum
- Add white wine and cream and cook two minutes or until sauce is brought back to boiling and add more salt and pepper to taste - **ENJOY!**

TIPS: Use part of the sauce to reheat fettuccini. I have made this dish with seafood as well and it is just as good.

Ted Nebbeling's Favourite

Ted Nebbeling, MLA, West Vancouver - Garibaldi, British Columbia, Minister of State for Community Charter

1 lb. pork tenderloin, veal or chicken breast
6 oz. mushrooms
2 cloves garlic
2 teaspoons capers and 2 teaspoons caper juice
12 leaves basil or 1 teaspoon basil paste
4 pieces sun dried tomatoes (soaked in hot water for ten minutes)
1/2 cup white wine
250 ml cream
Olive oil
1 tablespoon butter
Salt and pepper to taste
Fettuccini for 4

Cut meat in small pieces, slice mushrooms, chop garlic, cut sun dried tomatoes in small pieces, salt and pepper meat and dust with flour.

Cook fettuccini in rolling boiling water (do not overcook). Heat olive oil and butter in frying pan (make sure it is hot). Add meat and fry until brown. Simmer for 3 minutes stirring occasionally. Add sliced mushrooms and chopped garlic and simmer until most of the liquid has evaporated. Add capers, juice, sun dried tomatoes and basil. Stir and let cook on low heat for four minutes; bring heat back to maximum.

Add white wine and cream and cook two minutes or until sauce is brought back to boiling Add more salt and pepper to taste - Enjoy!

TIPS: Use part of the sauce to reheat fettuccini. I have made this dish with seafood as well and it is just as good.

"EASY TO PREPARE. I MADE TWO VERSIONS AT THE SAME TIME; ONE WITH CHICKEN AND ONE WITH JUST THE VEGETABLES. I RECOMMEND FRESH FRENCH BREAD TO MOP UP THE TASTY, RICH CREAM SAUCE."

– (TESTER) YASMIN JOHN-THORPE, WRITER AND COOKBOOK COMPILER.

Notes:

Province of
British Columbia
Legislative Assembly

Linda Reid, MLA (Richmond East)

Constituency Office:
130, 8040 Garden City Road
Richmond, B.C. V6Y 2N9
Phone: (604) 244-7343
Fax: (604) 775-1143

Official Opposition of British Columbia
Room 201
Parliament Buildings
Victoria, B.C. V8V 1X4
Phone: (250) 356-3056
Fax: (250) 387-2731

Mediterranean Lasagne

Ingredients

1 Medium Italian Sausage
2 Tbsp Olive Oil
1 Medium Onion
1 Tsp Oregano
1 Tub 475g Ricotta Cheese
½ Cup Parsley
6 Sheets No-Boil Lasagne
1 Med. Red & Green Pepper (chopped)
1 Jar 750ml Spaghetti Sauce
1/3 cup Black Olives Sliced
1/3 cup Parmesan Cheese
1 Egg
454 Grams Mozarella Cheese

Remove sausage from casing and crumble. In skillet, brown sausage in hot oil, add vegetables, cook 5 minutes, drain. Stir in sauce & oregano. Simmer, uncovered 10 minutes. Add Olives. Combine Ricotta, Parmesan, parsley and Egg. Slice 2/3 of Mozarella cheese and shred the remainder. In greased 13 x 9 pan place a thin layer of sauce. Top with 2 noodles. Spread with ½ each of the remaining ricotta mix and cheese slices. Cover with noodles then remaining ricotta mix and cheese slices. Top with 2 noodles and remaining sauce. Sprinkle with shredded mozarella cheese. Cover with lightly greased foil. Bake 350 degrees for 50-60 minutes or until bubbling. Uncover and cook for 5-10 minutes. Let stand 10 minutes before serving. Makes 8 servings.

Linda Reid

Linda Reid, MLA
Richmond East

Mediterranean Lasagne

Linda Reid, MLA, Richmond East,British Columbia, Minister of State for Early Childhood Development

1 medium Italian sausage
2 tablespoons olive oil
1 medium onion, chopped
1 teaspoon oregano
1 tub (475g) ricotta cheese
1/2 cup parsley
6 sheets no-boil lasagne
1 medium red pepper, chopped
1 medium green pepper, chopped
1 jar (750ml) spaghetti sauce
1/3 cup black olives, sliced
1/3 cup parmesan cheese
1 egg
1 pound (454g) mozzarella cheese

Remove sausage from casing and crumble. In skillet, brown sausage in hot oil, add vegetables, cook 5 minutes, drain. Stir in sauce and oregano. Simmer, uncovered 10 minutes. Add olives. Remove from heat. Combine ricotta, parmesan, parsley and egg. Slice 2/3 of mozzarella cheese and shred the remainder. In greased 9" x 13" pan place a thin layer of sauce. Top with 2 noodles. Spread with 1/2 each of the remaining ricotta mix and cheese slices. Cover with noodles then remaining ricotta mix and cheese slices. Top with 2 noodles and remaining sauce. Sprinkle with shredded mozarella cheese. Cover with lightly greased foil. Bake 350°F for 50-60 minutes or until bubbling. Uncover and cook 5-10 minutes. Let stand 10 minutes before serving. Makes 8 servings.

"I USED 1 POUND HOT ITALIAN SAUSAGES (PACKAGE OF 6) AND FRESH OREGANO. I ALSO USED A 7" X 11" BAKING DISH AND 9 SHEETS (3 PER LAYER) LASAGNE. I SPOONED SAUCE ON EACH LAYER BEFORE THE RICOTTA MIX AND CHEESE. EASY RECIPE TO FOLLOW."

– (TESTER) YASMIN JOHN-THORPE, WRITER AND COOKBOOK COMPILER.

Notes:

Province of
British Columbia
Legislative Assembly

OFFICIAL OPPOSITION

April Sanders, M.L.A.
(Okanagan-Vernon)

Constituency Office: 106 - 3334 — 30th Avenue, Vernon, B.C. V1T 2C8
Telephone: (250) 260-4474 Fax: (250) 549-5495
e-mail: aprils@vernon.com

Parliament Buildings, Victoria, B.C. V8V 1X4
Telephone: (250) 387-2746 Fax: (250) 387-2749

Chicken Crescent Wreath

2 tubes refrigerated croissant rolls (8 oz. Each or 4 croissants per roll)
1 cup of shredded cheddar cheese mixed together with
1 cup of shredded mozzarella cheese
1 tin condensed cream of celery or cream of chicken soup
1 cup chopped fresh broccoli
½ cup chopped sweet red peppers
1 tin chopped water chestnuts
1 – 1 ½ cup cubed cooked chicken
½ chopped white medium sized onion
1 tsp. Chopped dill

Arrange croissant rolls in a 12 inch pizza pan forming a ring with pointed ends facing out and wide ends overlapping. Combine the remaining ingredients. Spoon over wide ends of rolls. Fold points over filling and tuck under wide ends. (Filling will be visible). Bake at 375 degrees for 20 – 25 minutes or until golden brown. If top browns before bottom has cooked, cover temporarily with tin foil. Leftovers can be sliced up and reheated in the microwave at 50% power for easy lunches.

April Sanders

Chicken Crescent Wreath

April Sanders, Former MLA, Okanagan–Vernon, British Columbia

2 tubes refrigerated croissant rolls (8 oz. each or 4 croissants per roll)
1 cup shredded cheddar cheese mixed together with
1 cup shredded mozzarella cheese
1 tin condensed cream of celery or cream of chicken soup
1 cup chopped fresh broccoli
1/2 cup chopped sweet red peppers
1 tin chopped water chestnuts
1-1 1/2 cups cubed cooked chicken
1/2 chopped white medium- sized onion
1 teaspoon chopped dill

Notes:

Arrange croissant rolls on a 12″ pizza pan forming a ring with pointed ends facing out and wide ends overlapping. Combine the remaining ingredients. Spoon over wide ends of rolls. Fold points over filling and tuck under wide ends. (Filling will be visible.) Bake at 375°F for 20–25 minutes or until golden brown. If top browns before bottom has cooked, cover temporarily with tin foil. Leftovers can be sliced up and reheated in the microwave at 50% power for easy lunches.

"Quick and easy to make. Tasty. Great way to get kids to eat broccoli. I suggest the use of Jumbo size crescent rolls."

– (Tester) Ralph H. Kordass C.C.C., head chef Magnum's on the Lake Restaurant, Lakeside Resort and Casino.

HOUSE OF COMMONS
OTTAWA, CANADA
K1A 0A6

OTTAWA OFFICE
House of Commons
Room 409-S
Ottawa, Ontario
K1A 0A6
Tel: (613) 996-6740
Fax: (613) 947-0310
E-mail: Day.S@parl.gc.ca

CONSTITUENCY OFFICE
203-301 Main Street
Penticton, B.C.
V2A 5B7
Tel: (250) 770-4480
Fax: (250) 770-4484

STOCKWELL DAY, M.P.
Okanagan-Coquihalla
Leader of the Opposition

STOCKWELL DAY RIGHT WINGS

Quote: *"Choose your wings carefully. Right wings are reliable and contain the needed substance—they're tasty too. Left wings flop around quite a bit and have no taste at all."*

3lbs wings
½ cup Soy sauce
½ tsp Garlic poser (or ½ clove minced)
¼ cup Bulls Eye BBQ Sauce
½ cup Water

"Though this looks like a mixture of diverse groups, when they come together it's an exciting Alliance of flavour that really gets the juices going."

Place foil-lined baking sheet with wings into an oven at 350° for 30 minutes (until tender).
Drain off fat.
Pour sauce mixture over wings carefully. (remember, portions that are too Liberal can make you loose your appetite.)
Bake, uncovered, for 15 minutes.
Remove wings from oven. (This results in an irresistible 'stock')
Cool for five minutes
Place wings on a serving platter

All in all, I think this recipe will make your Day.

Stockwell Day

Stockwell Day Right Wings

Stockwell Day, MP, Okanagan-Coquihalla, British Columbia, Leader of the Official Opposition

3 pounds wings
1/2 cup soy sauce
1/2 teaspoon garlic poser (or 1/2 clove, minced)
1/4 cup Bulls Eye BBQ Sauce
1/2 cup water

"Though this looks like a mixture of diverse groups, when they come together it's an exciting Alliance of flavour that really gets the juices going."

Place foil-lined baking sheet with wings into an oven at 350°F for 30 minutes (until tender).

Drain off fat.

Pour sauce mixture over wings carefully. (Remember, portions that are too Liberal can make you lose your appetite.)

Bake, uncovered, for 15 minutes.

Remove wings from oven. (This results in an irresistible 'stock'.)

Cool for 5 minutes.

Place wings on a serving platter.

"I SUGGEST REDUCING THE SOYA SAUCE BY HALF TO LIGHTEN THE FLAVOUR, AS THE STAFF FELT THE SOYA FLAVOUR WAS TOO STRONG WHEN WINGS WERE DONE."

– (TESTER) RALPH H. KORDASS C.C.C., HEAD CHEF MAGNUM'S ON THE LAKE RESTAURANT, LAKESIDE RESORT AND CASINO.

Notes:

"Choose your wings carefully. Right wings are reliable and contain the needed substance – they're tasty too. Left wings flog around quite a bit and have no taste at all. All in all, I think this recipe will make your Day."

MEMORANDUM

TO: Yasmin John-Thorpe

FROM: Ann Marie Muss

DATE: February 8, 2000

SUBJECT: "TAKING THE HEAT: *Canadian Politicians in the Kitchen*"

Dear Mrs. John-Thorpe:

Senator Fitzpatrick has asked that I forward the attached recipe "Senator's Spare Ribs" for use in your Cookbook to be titled "TAKING THE HEAT: *Canadian Politicians in the Kitchen*". Also enclosed is a photograph of Senator Fitzpatrick. Senator Fitzpatrick is working on a quote, which will be provided to you.

I understand you have extended your deadline so perhaps there may be enough time for the Senator to have a photo taken of himself preparing the dish. I will follow-up with the Senator and let you know.

Please call or send a fax if you have any questions.

Yours Sincerely,

Ann Marie Muss,
Secretary to The Honourable D. Ross Fitzpatrick
(Kelowna Office)

Suite 802 - 1708 Dolphin Avenue - Kelowna, British Columbia - V1Y 9S4 - Phone: (250) 868-8019 - Fax: (250) 868-0829

Senator's Spare Ribs

Senator D. Ross Fitzpatrick, Kelowna, British Columbia

2 strips pork back ribs, cut into 3 or 4 rib pieces
1 onion, sliced into thin rings
1 bottle Kraft Regular BarBQ sauce
1 bottle Cedarcreek Estate Winery Pinot Noir
Salt

Notes:

Heat oven to 450°F. Place ribs in a single layer in pan and lightly sprinkle with salt. Place uncovered in oven and bake for 35 minutes. Remove ribs from oven, place ribs on paper towel to drain fat and wipe fat from pan.

Reduce oven to 375°F.

Replace ribs in pan, meaty side up. Mix 1/2 cup Kraft BarBQ sauce and 1/2 cup CedarCreek Pinot Noir. Pour half the mixture over ribs. Spread onion rings over ribs. Pour remaining mixture over ribs. Add 1/2 spoon of Kraft BarBQ sauce to each rib piece.

Cover pan with foil and return to oven for 2 hours, basting at 30-minute intervals for the first 1 1/2 hours (this is a good time to add baking potatoes to oven if you wish).

Last 1/2 hour remove foil, baste, add 1/2 spoon Kraft BarBQ sauce to each rib piece. Baste again in 15 minutes... 15 minutes later... melt-in-your-mouth ribs!

"EASY TO FOLLOW. I'M A REAL GARLIC FAN, SO I WOULD SUGGEST ADDING SOME CLOVES TO MAKE A MORE FLAVOURFUL SAUCE."

– (TESTER) PATRICIA MATEJU, CHOIR MEMBER.

"Serve with baked potato, Okanagan fresh steamed vegetables and of course the remaining Cedar Creek Pinot Noir."

PENNE WITH SPICY SAUSAGE

Ingredients

1 lb. hot Italian sausage (remove meat from casings)
2 tbsp. olive oil
1 large onion chopped
1 clove garlic minced
1 28 oz. can plum tomatoes (puréed)
¼ tsp. oregano
2 tbsp. dried basil or ¼ cup of fresh
2 tbsp. parsley
salt and pepper to taste (optional)
¼ cup fresh grated Parmesan cheese
5-6 cups penne

Method

Heat oil in fry pan. Add onions and garlic and sauté for 3-5 minutes. Add sausage meat and break with fork. Cook until sausage is slightly brown. Stir in puréed tomatoes and herbs. Simmer, uncovered for 25 minutes. Boil water and cook penne until al dente. Drain pasta when done, but don't rinse.

In large bowl, add grated Parmesan cheese to pasta. Pour sausage mix on top and stir. Serve immediately.

Serves 4-6 people.

With the compliments
Of Minnie Bonneot
Office of the Honourable Paul Martin, M.P.
La Salle-Émard

Ottawa
Tel: (613) 992-4284
Fax: (613) 992-4291

Riding
Tel: (514) 363-0954
Fax: (514) 367-5533

Penne with Spicy Sausage

Paul Martin, MP, La Salle-Émard, Quebec, Minister of Finance

Notes:

1 pound hot Italian sausage (remove meat from casings)
2 tablespoons olive oil
1 large onion, chopped
1 clove garlic, minced
1 28–ounce can plum tomatoes (puréed)
1/4 teaspoon oregano
2 tablespoons dried basil or 1/4 cup fresh
2 tablespoons parsley
Salt and pepper to taste (optional)
1/4 cup fresh grated Parmesan cheese
5-6 cups penne

Heat oil in fry pan. Add onions and garlic and sauté for 3-5 minutes. Add sausage meat and break with fork. Cook until sausage is slightly brown. Stir in puréed tomatoes and herbs. Simmer uncovered, for 25 minutes. Boil water and cook penne until al dente. Drain pasta when done, but don't rinse.

In a large bowl, add grated Parmesan cheese to pasta. Pour sausage mix on top and stir. Serve immediately.

Serves 4–6 people.

"Easy to prepare. No leftovers."

– (Tester) Yasmin John-Thorpe, writer and cookbook compiler.

"Very tasty. Hot and spicy. I like his great basic 'common sense' appeal to his meal. I highly recommend this dish."

– (Taster) Honourable Minister Rick Thorpe, MLA Okanagan/Westside.

OTTAWA OFFICE
ROOM 249 WEST BLOCK
OTTAWA, ONTARIO
K1A 0A6
TEL: (613) 996-4974
FAX: (613) 996-9749
E-MAIL: spellb@parl

HOUSE OF COMMONS
CANADA

BOB SPELLER, M.P.
Haldimand-Norfolk-Brant

CONSTITUENCY OFFICE
25 NORFOLK ST.N.
SIMCOE, ONTARIO
N3Y 3N6
TEL: (519) 426-9290
or 1-800-265-2825
FAX: (519) 426-5081

November 25, 1999

Ms. Yasmin John-Thorpe
150 Adamson Court
Pentiction, B.C.
V2A 7R8

Dear Ms. John-Thorpe:

Please find enclosed a copy of a family recipe, newspaper article and a small photo as you requested for your cookbook.

Please feel free to use my recipe and good luck in "Taking the Heat".

Yours sincerely,

Bob Speller, M.P.
Haldimand-Norfolk-Brant

PARLIAMENTARY SECRETARY TO THE MINISTER OF INTERNATIONAL TRADE

Veal (or Chicken) Scallopini (with sun-dried tomato sauce) over Fettuccine

Bob Speller, MP, Haldimand-Norfolk-Brant, Ontario

12 ounces fettuccine
1/2 cup sun-dried tomatoes
12 ounces veal scallopini or chicken, cut into thin strips
Sauce:
2 teaspoons olive oil
2 tablespoons crushed garlic
1 cup chopped onion
8 ounces sliced mushrooms
2/3 cup chicken or beef broth
2/3 cup 2% milk
1/3 cup dry white wine
1 1/4 cups tomato sauce
1/4 cup grated Parmesan cheese
Parsley

Notes:

Pour boiling water over sun-dried tomatoes. Let soak for 15 minutes. Drain and chop. Set aside. Cook pasta in boiling water according to package instructions. Drain and place in serving bowl. In a large non-stick skillet sprayed with vegetable spray, sauté veal until browned, approximately 5 minutes. Add to pasta. Make the sauce. Add oil to same skillet sprayed again with vegetable spray. Sauté garlic and onions until soft, approximately 4 minutes. Add mushrooms and sauté approximately 5 minutes. Add broth, milk, wine, tomato sauce and sun-dried tomatoes. Simmer on low heat for 12 minutes, stirring occasionally. Pour over pasta. Sprinkle with cheese and parsley and toss.

"This recipe is excellent."

- (Tester/Taster) Wendy Bosma, owner Gun Barrel Grill Restaurant.

HOUSE OF COMMONS
CANADA

The Honourable Lyle Vanclief, P.C.
MP for Prince Edward - Hastings

Sept. 26, 2000

Yasmin John-Thorpe
150 Adamson Ct.
Penticton BC V2A 7R8

Dear Yasmin,

The Minister asked that we send you this recipe as per your request for your cookbook "Taking the Heat".

I have included his pork marinade and chicken marinade recipes (they are pretty good!) along with the Minister's photograph, and a copy of an article that was in the Ottawa Citizen recently.

Best of luck with your book!

Best regards,

Bruce Knutson
Assistant to Hon. Lyle Vanclief, P.C., M.P.
Prince Edward-Hastings

Room 356
Confederation Building
House of Commons
Ottawa, Ontario K1A 0A6
613-992-5321
Fax (613) 996-8652
e-mail: vancll0@ parl.gc.ca

55 S. Front Street
Belleville, Ontario
K8N 5P4
613-969-7466
Fax (613) 969-7084

Pork Marinade

Lyle Vanclief, MP, Prince Edward–Hastings, Ontario, Minister of Agriculture

1 cup apple juice
1/2 cup soya sauce
2 tablespoons honey (liquid)
2 tablespoons canola oil
2 tablespoons garlic powder

Notes:

Marinate 6 butterfly pork chops (1″ thick) for several hours, or overnight. Barbecue.

"Easy to prepare. The taste is very mild."

– (Tester) Fay Rothlander, writer.

Chicken Marinade

2 tablespoons lemon juice
2 tablespoons olive oil
1/2 tablespoon salt
1/2 tablespoon pepper
1/4 tablespoon cumin
1/4 tablespoon oregano
2 cloves garlic, chopped

Marinate 1 pound boneless, skinless chicken breast for at least 2 hours in the refrigerator. Barbecue.

"This is easy to prepare. It gave the chicken a very interesting taste. I will gladly repeat this in my own cooking. A recipe to keep."

– (Tester) Fay Rothlander, writer.

"These recipes appeared in The Ottawa Citizen, *September 2000."*

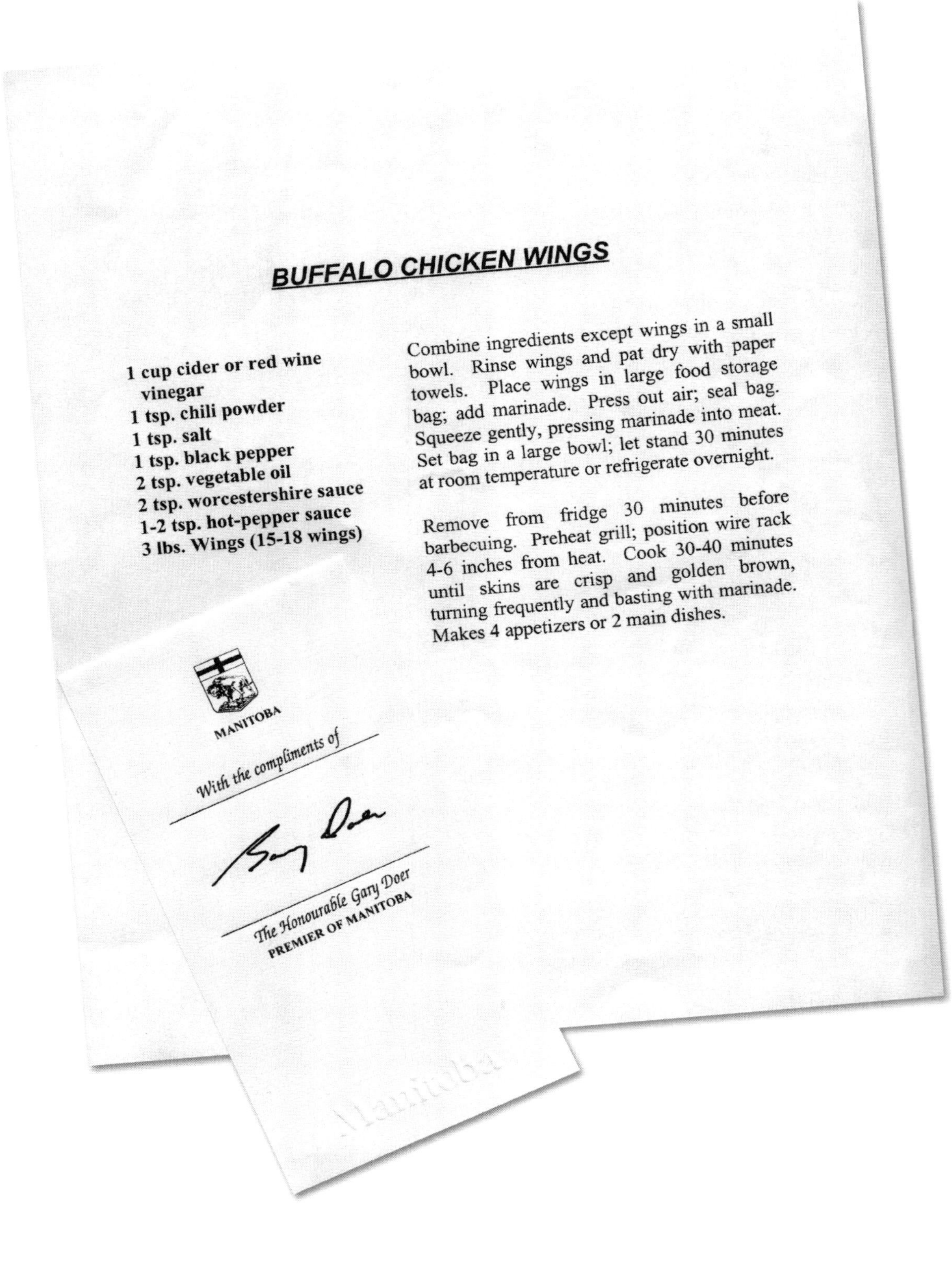

BUFFALO CHICKEN WINGS

1 cup cider or red wine vinegar
1 tsp. chili powder
1 tsp. salt
1 tsp. black pepper
2 tsp. vegetable oil
2 tsp. worcestershire sauce
1-2 tsp. hot-pepper sauce
3 lbs. Wings (15-18 wings)

Combine ingredients except wings in a small bowl. Rinse wings and pat dry with paper towels. Place wings in large food storage bag; add marinade. Press out air; seal bag. Squeeze gently, pressing marinade into meat. Set bag in a large bowl; let stand 30 minutes at room temperature or refrigerate overnight.

Remove from fridge 30 minutes before barbecuing. Preheat grill; position wire rack 4-6 inches from heat. Cook 30-40 minutes until skins are crisp and golden brown, turning frequently and basting with marinade. Makes 4 appetizers or 2 main dishes.

MANITOBA

With the compliments of

The Honourable Gary Doer
PREMIER OF MANITOBA

Manitoba

Buffalo Chicken Wings

Gary Doer, MLA, Concordia, Premier of Manitoba

Notes:

1 cup cider or red wine vinegar
1 teaspoon chili powder
1 teaspoon salt
1 teaspoon black pepper
2 teaspoons vegetable oil
2 teaspoons Worchestershire sauce
1-2 teaspoons hot-pepper sauce
3 pounds wings (15-18 wings)

Combine ingredients except wings in a small bowl. Rinse wings and pat dry with paper towels. Place wings in large food storage bag; add marinade. Press out air; seal bag. Squeeze gently, pressing marinade into meat. Set bag in a large bowl; let stand 30 minutes at room temperature or refrigerate overnight.

Remove from fridge 30 minutes before barbecuing. Preheat grill; position wire rack 4-6 inches from heat. Cook 30-40 minutes until skins are crisp and golden brown, turning frequently and basting with marinade.

Makes 4 appetizers or 2 main dishes.

"Reduce the amount of vinegar, as I found it to be a little too tart. Also, I cannot recommend using the marinade for basting. This is a food safety issue (salmonella)."

– (Tester) Ralph H. Kordass C.C.C., head chef Magnum's on the Lake Restaurant, Lakeside Resort and Casino.

Hon. Bernard Lord
Premier / Premier ministre

New Nouveau Brunswick

April 12, 2000

Ms. Yasmin John-Thorpe
150 Adamson Court
Penticton BC V2A 7R8

Dear Ms. John-Thorpe :

As my contribution to your cookbook titled *Taking the Heat: Canadian Politicians in the Kitchen*, I am pleased to share the recipe for a dish I most enjoy. It is called *Premier's Beef Bourguignon* and is a favourite among many family members and friends.

Also enclosed, you will find a picture as requested to accompany the recipe.

I wish you much success in the publication and sale of your book and commend you for your generosity in contributing some of the proceeds to the food banks.

Sincerely,

Bernard Lord

Tel./Téléphone :
(506) 453-2144
Fax/Télécopieur :
(506) 453-7407
E-Mail/Courriel :
premier@gov.nb.ca

P.O. Box 6000
Fredericton
New Brunswick
Canada E3B 5H1

Case postale 6000
Fredericton
Nouveau-Brunswick
Canada E3B 5H1

Premier's Beef Bourguignon

Bernard Lord, MLA, Moncton East, Premier of New Brunswick

3 1/2 pounds blade roast, cut into 1 1/2 inch cubes
2 tablespoons corn oil
1 tablespoon butter
Salt and pepper to taste
2 tablespoons butter
1 Spanish onion, chopped
3 garlic cloves, finely chopped
1 teaspoon thyme
3 bay leaves
4 tablespoons flour
1 1/2 cups dry red wine
1 1/2 cups hot beef broth
1/2 pound mushrooms, cut in large pieces
1 tablespoon fresh parsley

Preheat oven to 350°F.

Heat corn oil and 1 tablespoon butter in large deep frying pan. Brown beef cubes. Season with salt and pepper and set aside.

In another frying pan, melt 2 tablespoons butter. Add onion and cook 2–3 minutes. Add garlic, thyme and bay leaves and cook another 2 minutes.

Sprinkle beef cubes with the flour. Return the beef to heat. While stirring, cook over medium heat for 4–5 minutes.

Add the onion and seasoning mixture. Pour all in a deep casserole. Cover and cook in oven for 1 1/2 hours or until beef is very tender.

Add mushrooms and parsley and cook another 15 minutes.

"Easy recipe to follow. Really good."

– (Tester/Taster) Wendy Bosma, owner Gun Barrel Grill Restaurant.

Notes:

"I am pleased to share the recipe for a dish I most enjoy. It is called Premier's Beef Bourguignon and is a favourite among many family members and friends."

HOUSE OF ASSEMBLY
NEWFOUNDLAND AND LABRADOR

There is nothing I enjoy more than having family and friends drop in for dinner. Invitations are never needed `*who so ever will may come*'. Sometimes so many arrive it's similar to the parable of the ***'Loaves and Fishes'***.

Other times one might wonder what to do with so much food. Regardless of the crew everyone gets fed and seldom is there any leftovers.

I especially enjoy cooking this meal at my cabin with the aroma drawing in all visitors to the Garnish Pond. This meal combined with a few refreshments, some guitar music and a sing along leads to an enjoyable evening.

I want to wish you all the best on the success of your cookbook..

Sincerely,

Mary Hodder, MHA
Burin-Placentia West

Government Members Office, 3rd. Floor, East Block., Confederation Building, P.O. Box 8700, St. John's, Newfoundland, Canada, A1B 4J6

Mary Hodder's Company's Coming Turkey & Dressing

Mary Hodder, MHA, Burin–Placentia West, Newfoundland and Labrador, Deputy Chair of Committees

Allow approximately 1 cup of dressing per 2 pounds of turkey. Day old bread is best.

6–8 cups bread crumbs
1 large chopped onion
Salt and pepper to taste
1/2 cup butter or margarine
4 teaspoons Newfoundland savoury

Bake stuffed turkey at 325°F, allowing 20 minutes per pound. Approximately 20 minutes before dinner is ready place paste over the turkey:

Paste

3 cups flour
3 tablespoons baking powder
1/4 teaspoon salt
1 tablespoon butter or margarine
3 tablespoons sugar

Rub all ingredients together. Add enough cold water to form a soft dough. Form into balls and place on top of turkey. Spoon some of the turkey drippings over the paste. Let cook for approximately 20 minutes.

Gravy

Remove turkey from roaster. Drain and discard grease. Add 3 or 4 cups of water from the boiled dinner (jigs dinner – see page 96). Add 1 onion cut in small pieces and 1 package of Knox chicken bouillon. Bring to a boil on top of the stove. Add a few drops of gravy browning for colour and add thickening. (To make gravy thickening, place 2 or 3 tablespoons of flour in a bottle with about 1/2 cup of cold water. Put cover tightly on bottle and shake until all flour is completely dissolved. Add to boiling gravy.) When gravy thickens remove from heat.

"I baked the turkey for the local Soup Kitchen. The balls made from the paste turned out to be like soda biscuits. Great hit with the kitchen regulars." Note: See Mary Hodder's other company's coming recipes appear on pages 96 and 128.

– (Tester) Yasmin John-Thorpe, writer and cookbook compiler.

Notes:

"There is nothing I enjoy more than having family and friends drop in for dinner. Invitations are never needed 'who so ever will may come'. Sometimes so many arrive it's similar to the parable of the 'Loaves and Fishes'."

Territoires du Nord-Ouest Assemblée législative

Steve Nitah's Moose Fritters
MLA Tu Nedhe
NWT Legislative Assembly

½ lb. Lard
Onion
Moose meat
1 box Kraft Dinner

Fry up moose chunks in lard and onion (marinate in apple juice optional).

Boil ~~K-D~~ water. Add macaroni. When ready, put in cheese and milk. Stir.

Mix together with moose chunks.

Dig in.

Not to be confused with Road Kill Café Recipes.

Quote: "Always fresh, always good."

Yellowknife, Territoires du Nord-Ouest, Canada, X1A 2L9 · Telécopieur: (403) 920-4735, tél.: (403) 873-7999

Steve Nitah's Moose Fritters

Steve Nitah, MLA, Tu Nedhe, North West Territories

1/2 pound lard
Onion, chopped
Moose meat
1 box Kraft Dinner

Notes:

Fry up moose chunks in lard and onion (optional – marinate in apple juice).

Boil water. Add macaroni. When ready, put in cheese and milk. Stir. Mix together with moose chunks.

Dig in.

Not to be confused with Road Kill Café Recipes.

"I used 2 pounds of Moose meat and half the lard. Recipe was very easy to prepare. I recommend this as a good hunting man's meal at camp."

– (Tester) Todd Romano, wild game hunter and power lineman, West Kootenay Power Ltd.

Compiler's note: My thanks to Father Wayne Pfliger, St. Ann's and St. John Vianney Parish Priest, who kindly donated moose meat from one of his hunting trips.

"Always fresh, always good."

THE PREMIER
HALIFAX, NOVA SCOTIA
B3J 2T3

November 2, 1999

Ms. Yasmin John-Thorpe
150 Adamson Court
Penticton, BC B2A 7R8

Dear Ms. John-Thorpe:

I am neither a gourmet cook, nor do I possess any qualities which would remotely resemble one. However, at your request, I am pleased to provide you with a fool-proof and uncomplicated favourite recipe which, on occasion, I have been brave enough to prepare for a small and carefully-selected group of family and friends.

To tie into your comment "You are what you eat", I am an uncomplicated, straight-forward and dependable person. These words accurately describe the recipe for Hamburg Soup as shown below.

1 ½ pounds of lean ground round
3 cans beef broth, or equivalent
2 cans water
1 28-oz can of stewed tomatoes, broken up
1 can tomato soup, undiluted
1 Bay Leaf, 1 T Oregano, 1 t Basil, Lemon Dill to taste
7 T pearl barley
4 carrots, diced
1 large onion, diced
3 stalks celery, diced
1 zucchini, diced

Method:
Cook lean ground, draining fat. Add all ingredients, except for zucchini, and let simmer for 1 ½ to 2 hours. During the final ½ hour, add the zucchini. This is a very hearty, full-body soup which, in a pinch, can be served as a full meal. Enjoy!

Ms. John-Thorpe, I wish you success with your project and look forward to seeing the published version of your cookbook – *Taking the Heat: Canadian Politicians in the Kitchen.*

Sincerely,

John Hamm

John F. Hamm

Enclosures (1)

Printed on paper that contains recycled fibre

Hamburg Soup

John F. Hamm, MLA, Pictou Centre, Premier of Nova Scotia

Notes:

1 1/2 pounds lean ground round beef
3 cans beef broth, or equivalent
2 cans water
1 28–ounce can stewed tomatoes, broken up
1 can tomato soup, undiluted
1 bay leaf
1 tablespoon oregano
1 teaspoon basil
Lemon dill to taste
7 tablespoons pearl barley
4 carrots, diced
1 large onion, diced
3 stalks celery, diced
1 zucchini, diced

Cook lean ground beef, draining fat. Add all ingredients, except for zucchini, and let simmer for 1 1/2 to 2 hours. During the final 1/2 hour, add the zucchini. This is a very hearty, full-bodied soup which, in a pinch, can be served as a full meal. Enjoy!

"HEARTY, FULL-BODIED SOUP. CAN BE MADE IN A SLOW COOKER. FOR VARIETY OMIT BASIL, OREGANO AND DILL AND USE 1/2 TSP. THYME AND FRESH GROUND PEPPER."

– (TESTER) JULIANNE BEAUCHAMP, MUSIC EDUCATOR.

"You are what you eat."

ᓯᕗᓪᓕᖅᑎ ᐹᓪ ᐅᑲᓕᖅ
Premier Paul Okalik
Paul Okalik, Premier ministre
Kavamat Havaktia Paul Okalik

September 7, 2000

Ms. Yasmin John-Thorpe
150 Adamson Court
PENTICTON, BC V2A 7R8

Dear Ms. John-Thorpe:

Please accept my apologies for the delay in responding to your request for my favorite recipe.

I have enclosed a copy of a recipe for Barbecue Caribou Burgers, along with some photos that you had requested. I certainly hope that everyone enjoys the recipe, I know I certainly do!

Once you have finished the production of this recipe book, be sure to let my staff know.

Yours truly,

ᐹᓪ ᐅᑲᓕᖅ

Paul Okalik

Enclosure

ᑎᑎᖅᑲᒃᑯᕕᒃ 800, ᐃᖃᓗᐃᑦ, ᓄᓇᕗᑦ X0A 0H0 ᑲᓇᑕ • Box 800, Iqaluit, Nunavut X0A 0H0 Canada

Barbecued Caribou Burger

Paul Okalik, MLA, Iqaluit East, Premier of Nunavut

Ground caribou meat
Barbecue sauce of choice

Combine ground caribou meat. Place patties on barbecue over medium coals. Grill uncovered 13–15 minutes to medium wellness, turning occasionally. Just before patties are done cooking, brush on your preferred barbecue sauce, as desired.

Prepare your bun as you please.

"I SEASONED CARIBOU STEAKS WITH SALT AND PEPPER. GRILLED ON VERY HOT BARBECUE FOR 3 MINUTES ON ONE SIDE AND FLIPPED OVER FOR 2 MINUTES ON THE OTHER SIDE. EASY MEAL. THE MEAT IS VERY MILD, LEAN AND TASTY."

– (TESTER) TODD ROMANO, WILD GAME HUNTER AND POWER LINEMAN, WEST KOOTENAY POWER LTD.

Notes:

"I certainly hope that everyone enjoys the recipe. I know I certainly do!"

The Premier of Ontario
Legislative Building
Queen's Park
Toronto, Ontario
M7A 1A1

Le Premier ministre de l'Ontario
Hôtel du gouvernement
Queen's Park
Toronto (Ontario)
M7A 1A1

Ontario

February 14, 2000

Ms. Yasmin John-Thorpe
150 Adamson Court
Penticton, British Columbia
V2A 7R8

Dear Ms. John-Thorpe:

I have received your e-mail message and am pleased to provide you with my favourite recipe for beef stew. It's easy to prepare, nutritious, and quite popular with my two growing boys.

I wish you all the best with your book.

Sincerely,

Michael D. Harris, MPP

Enclosures

Beef Stew

Michael D. Harris, MPP, Nipissing, Premier of Ontario

1 pound stewing beef
12 small potatoes
4 carrots, sliced
1 1/2 cups turnip, chopped
3 onions, sliced
3 stalks celery, chopped
1/4 cup all-purpose flour
3/4 teaspoon dried marjoram
2 cups beef stock
1 tablespoon tomato paste
1 bay leaf
Salt and pepper

Cut beef into bite-sized cubes, trimming all fat. Combine beef, carrots, turnip, onions and celery in ovenproof casserole. Sprinkle with flour and stir in stock, tomato paste and marjoram, add bay leaf. Cover and bake in a 325°F oven for 1 hour. Add potatoes, cover and bake for 75 minutes until potatoes are tender. Discard bay leaf, season with salt and pepper to taste.

Makes 6 servings.

"I WAS PLEASANTLY SURPRISED THAT THE BEEF DID NOT REQUIRE PRE-BROWNING. THE FINISHED STEW HAD A NICE RICH BROWN SAUCE – QUITE TASTY."

– (TESTER) RALPH H. KORDASS C.C.C., HEAD CHEF MAGNUM'S ON THE LAKE RESTAURANT, LAKESIDE RESORT AND CASINO.

Notes:

"This recipe is easy to prepare, nutritious and quite popular with my two growing boys."

Prince Edward Island

Legislative Assembly

Office of the Speaker
PO Box 2000
Charlottetown
Prince Edward Island
Canada C1A 7N8

Tel 902 368 4310
Fax 902 368 5175
http://www.gov.pe.ca/

November 25, 1999

Yasmin John-Thorpe
150 Adamson Court
Penticton, B.C. V2A 7R8

Dear Mrs. John-Thorpe:

I am sending you a recipe for Hon. Wilbur MacDonald, Speaker of the Legislative Assembly of Prince Edward Island. I am also enclosing a picture of the Speaker.

I hope I am not too late in sending this. This cookbook sounds like a great idea and good luck with it.

Sincerely,

Barbara O'Donnell
Secretary to the Speaker

Hamburg Casserole

Wilbur MacDonald, MLA, Belfast–Pownalbay, Speaker of the Legislative Assembly, Prince Edward Island

1 pound ground beef
1 small onion, chopped
1/2 green pepper, chopped
1/2 cup celery, chopped
1 284 ml tin mushrooms (bits & pieces)
1 tablespoon Mazola oil

Notes:

Cook all in fry pan for about 5 minutes.

Cook 1/2 package broad noodles. Drain and add to pan.

Add:
1 can tomatoes
1 small can tomato paste
1 garlic clove or garlic salt
Salt and pepper to taste

Toss and put in casserole with grated cheese on top. Bake 45 minutes at 350°F.

"Easy to prepare. Made for the Rotary Fundraiser Dinner. No left-overs."

– (Tester) Yasmin John-Thorpe, writer and cookbook compiler.

"This is so tasty."

– (Tester) Laurel Reitlo, past president Rotary Anns, Penticton.

Prince Edward Island **Île-du-Prince-Édouard**

Legislative Assembly

Assemblée législative

PARVA SUB INGENTI

Tel 902 368 4360
Fax 902 368 4377
www.gov.pe.ca/

Government Members' Office
PO Box 338
Charlottetown
Prince Edward Island
Canada C1A 7K7

Bureau des députés provinciaux
C.P. 338
Charlottetown
Île-du-Prince-Édouard
Canada C1A 7K7

Tél. : 902 368 4360
Téléc. : 902 368 4377
www.gov.pe.ca/

March 30, 2001

Ms. Yasmine John-Thorpe
150 Adamson Court
Penticton, BC V2A 7R8

Dear Ms. John-Thorpe:

Thank you for asking me to include my favourite recipe in your cookbook.

I love any kind of a chicken meal, but I am especially fond of this recipe for Japanese Chicken Wings. This recipe is quick and easy to prepare and has a little spice to it. I'm sure everyone will enjoy it as much as my family does.

My sincere best wishes for your success with "Taking the Heat: Canadian Politicians in the Kitchen."

Yours truly,

Elmer MacFadyen , MLA
District 10
Sherwood - Hillsborough

aah
Enclosure

Japanese Chicken Wings

Elmer MacFadyen, MLA, Sherwood-Hillsborough, Prince Edward Island, Government House Leader

3 pounds chicken wings
1 beaten egg
1 cup flour
1 cup butter

Notes:

Cut wings in half. Dip in slightly beaten egg and then in flour. Fry in butter until brown and crisp. Put in shallow roasting pan and pour sauce over wings.

Sauce:
3 tablespoons soya sauce
2 tablespoons water
1 cup white sugar
1/2 cup vinegar
1 teaspoon accent
1/2 teaspoon salt

Bake at 350°F for 30 minutes. Spoon sauce over wings during cooking.

"Very tasty. Tasted like a true Oriental dish."

– (Tester) Wendy Bosma, owner Gun Barrel Grill Restaurant.

"You are what you eat, and I enjoy eating."

Doreen Hamilton MLA
Regina Wascana Plains

Constituency Office
208 University Park Drive
Regina, SK
S4V 1A3
522-1027
fax 522-4992

April 28th, 2000

Ms. Yasmin John-Thorpe
150 Adamson Court
Penticton, British Columbia
V2A 7R8

Dear Ms. John-Thorpe;

I am writing to provide you with written permission to use the recipes I have already sent. It is my pleasure to be a part of your project.

I have also included a photo, which you may use with the recipes.

Please do not hesitate to get in touch with me if I may be of any further assistance.

I wish you the best of luck!

Sincerely,

Doreen E. Hamilton

Doreen E. Hamilton, MLA
Regina Wascana Plains

Lazy Cabbage Rolls

Doreen E. Hamilton, MLA, Regina Wascana Plains, Saskatchewan, Minister for Saskatchewan Property Management Corporation; Status of Women

2 large onions, chopped
1 pound ground beef
1 pound ground pork
1 small can Alpha (condensed) Milk
1 can tomato soup
1 1/2 cups uncooked rice
1 1/2 tablespoons salt
1/4 teaspoon pepper
1 large head cabbage

Notes:

Fry together the onions, beef and pork. Shred cabbage, fry until limp. Mix together and pour into a large casserole. Cover with 1 can tomato soup mixed with condensed milk. Bake 1 hour at 350°F. Freezes well.

"AN OLD FAVOURITE, ALWAYS PLEASING HEARTY FARE."

– (TESTER) SUE PREMACK, MEDICAL OFFICE ASSISTANT.

"Yesterday is already a dream,
And tomorrow is only a vision;
But today well-lived makes
Every yesterday
A dream of happiness
And every tomorrow a vision of hope."
– quote from the Sanskrit

HOW TO BARBEQUE A WILD CANADIAN GOOSE

First you have to go out and bag a goose or find a friend who will go hunting for one.

It is important to take the time to clean all the down and pin feathers.

The trick to tastiness is garlic and orange juice.

Insert at lease one clove of garlic into each breast and into each thigh.
Season the bird as you would any fowl. I use salt, pepper, paprika, cumin, curry and cinnamon.

To keep things simple for clean up I purchase a disposable aluminium roast pan and cover the goose with aluminium foil. However, a good roaster works well.

Keep the barbecue at low heat so as not to burn the pan too much. Start with a
little orange juice in the pan and continue to add orange juice as it evaporates.
Pour the juice over the bird to keep it moist. Use a fork to prick holes in the bird
to allow fat* to escape and orange juice to penetrate. Cook for a long time until
the bird appears to have shrunk. It can take from 6 to 9 hours depending on the
size of the bird to get a nice glaze on it. Good to have a spare tank of fuel around.

Cut the breasts out in one piece and slice them so every serving has some skin on
it. The skin is the delicacy. Some people like to make stuffing for birds. That's
another speciality, but it does take longer to cook a stuffed bird, so I keep it simple.
I usually toss in onions and parsnip.

It's nice to serve it with a slice or two of orange.

♦♦♦♦♦♦♦♦

* (P.S. Old Wive's Tale)
Goose grease has been used therapeutically for rough skin. It can be strained and
collected, applied to hands covered with plastic gloves and worn overnight to feel
the benefits.

M Kowalsky

Myron Kowalsky, MLA
Prince Albert Carlton
Prince Albert, Saskatchewan

Barbecued Wild Canadian Goose

Myron Kowalsky, MLA, Prince Albert–Carlton, Saskatchewan, Speaker of the House

First you have to go out and bag a goose or find a friend who will go hunting for one. It is important to take the time to clean all the down and pin feathers.

The trick to tastiness is garlic and orange juice. Insert at least one clove of garlic into each breast and into each thigh. Season the bird as you would any fowl. I use salt, pepper, paprika, cumin, curry and cinnamon.

To keep things simple for clean-up I purchase a disposable aluminium roast pan and cover the goose with aluminium foil. However, a good roaster works well.

Keep the barbecue at low heat so as not to burn the pan too much. Start with a little orange juice in the pan and continue to add orange juice as it evaporates. Pour the juice over the bird to keep it moist. Use a fork to prick holes in the bird to allow fat* to escape and orange juice to penetrate. Cook for a long time until the bird appears to have shrunk. It can take from 6–9 hours depending on the size of the bird to get a nice glaze on it. Good to have a spare tank of fuel around.

Cut the breasts out in one piece and slice them so every serving has some skin on it. The skin is the delicacy. Some people like to make stuffing for birds. That's another speciality, but it does take longer to cook a stuffed bird, so I keep it simple. I usually toss in onions and parsnips. It's nice to serve the meat with a slice or two of fresh orange.

(P.S. Old Wives Tale) Goose grease has been used therapeutically for rough skin. It can be strained and collected; apply to hands, cover with plastic gloves and wear overnight to feel the benefits.

"A WONDERFUL DISH. GOOSE CAN BE REALLY FATTY, TAKE TIME TO DRAIN OFF FAT DURING COOKING. TRY ON A ROTISSERIE – FAT AND JUICES SELF-BASTE THE BIRD."

– (TESTER) ROBERTA ROBERTSON, INTERIOR DECORATOR AND CHEF.

Notes:

"Be Happy and Pay Your Taxes."

Minister of Economic and
Co-operative Development

SASKATCHEWAN

Legislative Building
Regina, Saskatchewan S4S 0B3

APR 1 4 2000

Ms. Yasmin John-Thorpe
150 Adamson Court
PENTICTON BC V2A 7R8

Dear Ms. John-Thorpe:

Thank you for writing to me requesting a recipe and picture for your cookbook titled TAKING THE HEAT: *Canadian Politicians in the Kitchen.* I appreciate you including me in your interesting publication in this way.

I am pleased to provide you with a recipe for Mushroom and Ham Tarts. I have also enclosed a picture as you requested. As such, please accept my best wishes in your future endeavours.

Sincerely,

Janice

Janice MacKinnon

Mushroom and Ham Tarts

Janice MacKinnon, MLA, Saskatoon Idylwyld, Saskatchewan, Minister Economic and Co-operative Development

2 cups finely chopped mushrooms
1/2 cup chopped onion
1/4 cup butter
1 cup minced lean cooked ham
1/2 cup grated Swiss cheese
1/4 snipped fresh dill
or 3/4 teaspoon dried dill weed
Pepper
16 small unbaked tart shells

Notes:

Add mushrooms and onion to heated butter in skillet. Cover and cook over medium-low heat until very tender, 8-10 minutes. Uncover and continue cooking until accumulated liquid evaporates and mixture is just moist, 3–4 minutes, stirring often. Remove from heat. Stir in ham, cheese and dill. Season generously with pepper. Fill tart shells with mixture, dividing evenly. Bake at 425°F until pastry is golden and filling appears firm on top (10–15 minutes).

"Easy to prepare."

– (Tester) Roberta Robertson, interior decorator and chef.

"I found the tarts very tasteful, the perfect appetizer." "Recipe made lots more than 16 tarts." "Yummy!"

– (Tasters) Charlene Mercier's Bridal Shower guests.

Mary Hodder's Company's Coming Jigs Dinner

Mary Hodder, MHA, Burin–Placentia West, Newfoundland and Labrador, Deputy Chair of Committees

2 pieces vacuum–packed salt beef
1 head cabbage
1 large turnip
1 package carrots
5 pounds potatoes

Remove excess fat and place beef in cold water. Cook for 1 hour. Strain water (reserve a little of the water to place in pot with peas pudding). Half fill cooking pot with hot water. Continue to boil beef for another hour. Add cabbage, boil for another 20 minutes, add carrot and turnip and boil for another half hour. Add potatoes and cook until done – approximately half an hour. Add water as needed during cooking. (Use 3 – 4 cups for turkey gravy. See page 77)

"BROUGHT BACK MEMORIES OF MY YEARS IN NEWFOUNDLAND. EASY TO PREPARE AND A MUST FOR COLD RAINY FALL EVENINGS BEFORE A ROARING FIRE."

– (TESTER) YASMIN JOHN-THORPE, WRITER AND COOKBOOK COMPILER.

Mary Hodder's Company's Coming Peas Pudding

1 package split yellow peas
1/2 cup salt pork cubes

Soak 1 package split peas. Add 1/2 cup of salt pork cubes. Place in pudding bag and cook in a separate pot. Before placing pudding bag in pot, place a wire rack or a plate on the bottom of the pot to prevent bag from burning.

"I HAD NEVER MADE NEWFOUNDLAND'S PEAS PUDDING WITH SALT PORK CUBES BEFORE. RINSE PORK SEVERAL TIMES TO REMOVE EXCESS SALT. TASTY AND STILL ONE OF MY FAVOURITES."

– (TESTER) YASMIN JOHN-THORPE, WRITER AND COOKBOOK COMPILER.

DESSERTS

BRITISH COLUMBIA

July 6, 2001

Yasmin John-Thorpe
150 Adamson Court
Penticton, B.C.
V2A 7R8

Dear Yasmin:

Congratulations on your efforts to put together this great cookbook!

I look forward to having an opportunity to try out some of the intriguing recipes submitted by many elected officials from across the country.

You have done an excellent job and ultimately created a new and welcome addition to the collection of Canadiana books produced, printed, catalogued and sold in Canada.

I wish you all the best.

Sincerely,

Gordon Campbell
Premier

Office of the Premier

Mailing Address:
PO Box 9041 Stn Prov Govt
Victoria BC V8W 9E1

Location:
Parliament Buildings
Victoria

Peanut Butter Cookies

Gordon Campbell, MLA, Vancouver–Point Grey, Premier of British Columbia

1/2 cup Mazola oil
1/2 cup peanut butter
1/4 cup white sugar
1/3 cup brown sugar
1/2 teaspoon vanilla
1 egg
1/2 teaspoons salt
1/2 teaspoon cream of tartar
1 1/2 cup flour

Mix Mazola and peanut butter. Cream together sugars, vanilla and egg; add to Mazola and peanut butter mixture. Add remaining ingredients.

Roll into balls and place on ungreased baking sheet. Using a fork, press lightly to flatten the cookie. Bake at 400°F 10-12 minutes.

Additions: You can add chocolate chips, peanuts, etc., to give a different flavour.

"An efficient, effective little cookie, which is quite delectable. Easy on the pocketbook to make – a great value. Unpretentious but you'll definitely come back for more!"

– (Tester) Judy Lloyd, President Rotary Anns Penticton.

Notes:

"It goes without saying, but, it goes a lot better with saying."

Farnworth, Mike (Office) Mike.Farnworth.Office@leg.bc.ca
Thursday, October 07, 1999 9:44 AM
RE: Taking the Heat

Per your request

Mike Farnworth, MLA

Favorite Chocolate Cake

¾ cup cocoa powder
½ cup boiling water
3 sticks butter
2 ¼ cups sugar
1 T. vanilla
1 cup milk
4 eggs
3 cups all-purpose flour
1 tsp. baking soda

Whisk together the cocoa powder and boiling water. Cream together the butter and sugar until light and fluffy in a separate bowl. Add the vanilla and eggs one at a time, mixing well. Mix together the cocoa mixture and the milk. To the egg mixture, alternately add the milk, cocoa and flour. Finally, mix in the baking soda. Pour the batter evenly into three cake pans. Bake at 350 degrees for 40-45 minutes.

Frosting

In a large bowl, combine the ingredients with an electric mixer until smooth. Add more milk if necessary, until frosting is fluffy and spreadable. Place cake on platter. Spread with frosting in layers.

Favourite Chocolate Cake

Mike Farnworth, Former MLA, Port Coquitlam, British Columbia

3/4 cup cocoa powder
1/2 cup boiling water
3 sticks butter
2 1/4 cups sugar
1 teaspoon vanilla
1 cup milk
4 eggs
3 cups all-purpose flour
1 teaspoon baking soda

Whisk together the cocoa powder and boiling water. Cream together the butter and sugar until light and fluffy in a separate bowl. Add the vanilla and eggs one at a time, mixing well. Mix together the cocoa mixture and the milk. To the egg mixture, alternately add the milk, cocoa and flour. Finally, mix in the baking soda. Pour the batter evenly into three greased cake pans. Bake at 350°F for 40–45 minutes.

Frosting

4 cups icing sugar
3-4 tablespoons cocoa
1/3 cup butter (soft)
4-6 tablespoons milk
1 teaspoon vanilla

In a large bowl, combine the ingredients with an electric mixer until smooth. Add more milk if necessary, until frosting is fluffy and spreadable. Place cake on platter. Spread with frosting in layers. Stack layers and frost entire cake.

"FULL–BODIED CAKE. DON'T OVERBAKE AS IT CAN DRY OUT."

– (TESTER) JANELLE BREESE-BIAGIONI, AUTHOR.

Notes:

GOVERNMENT OF
NEWFOUNDLAND AND LABRADOR

Treasury Board
Office of the Minister

11 January 2000

Ms. Yasmin John-Thorpe
150 Adamson Court
Penticton, British Columbia
V2A 7R8

Dear Ms. John-Thorpe:

Thank you for your recent note, and I look forward to purchasing the "Taking the Heat" cook book. Please let me know when they will be available.

By the way, Wayne Thistle is a cousin of by husband, and I know both Wayne & Gloria very well.

Many thanks and best wishes for 2000.

Yours sincerely,

Anna Thistle, MHA
Grand Falls-Buchans District
President of Treasury Board

P.O. Box 8700, St. John's, Newfoundland, Canada, A1B 4J6, Telephone (709) 729-2858, Facsimile (709) 729-6791

Bakeapple Torte

Anna Thistle, MHA, Grand Falls–Buchans, Newfoundland and Labrador, Minister of Labour

Base:

4 eggs
1 cup sugar
1 cup Graham Wafer crumbs
1 teaspoon baking powder
1 cup chopped walnuts

Separate eggs. Beat 4 egg whites with 1/2 cup sugar until stiff – set aside.

Beat 4 egg yolks with 1/2 cup sugar. Add Graham Wafer crumbs, combined with baking powder. Fold in egg whites and nuts.

Bake in greased 10″ spring form pan at 325˚F for 45 minutes. Cool in pan on a cake rack.

Topping:

2 cups fresh or frozen bakeapples
1/2 - 3/4 cups water
3/4 cups sugar
1 package Dream Whip (prepared as per package instructions) or 1 pint of fresh whipping cream

Bring berries and water to a rolling boil and boil for 5 minutes. Add 3/4 cup sugar – continue to boil for another 5 minutes. Let cool.

Fold berries into Dream Whip or cream. Spread berry mixture on Torte and serve.

Variation: Bakeapples may be substituted with any fresh berry, e.g., raspberries, strawberries, blueberries.

"EASY TO MAKE. NO NEWFOUNDLAND BAKEAPPLE BERRIES, SO I SUBSTITUTED STRAWBERRIES."

– (TESTER) BEVERLEY GARTNER, CHILDREN'S WRITER AND SPIRITUAL HEALER.

"MY FAMILY ENJOYED THIS DESSERT, ESPECIALLY THE TOPPING."

– (TASTERS) GARTNER FAMILY

Notes:

"A delightful Newfoundland and Labrador dessert."

GOVERNMENT OF
NEWFOUNDLAND AND LABRADOR

Department of
Development and
Rural Renewal
Office of the Minister

October 7, 1999

Ms. Yasmin John-Thorpe
1500 Adamson Street
Penticton, British Columbia
V2A 7R8

Dear Mrs. John-Thorpe:

Please find enclosed a recipe that I often prepare for my family and friends.

I am pleased to contribute a recipe to your cookbook and I hope you are able to have your manuscript ready before Christmas 1999.

Once again, good luck and all the best in your commendable endeavour!

Sincerely,

Beaton Tulk

BEATON TULK, M.H.A.
Minister
GOVERNMENT HOUSE LEADER

P.O. Box 8700, St. John's, Newfoundland, Canada, A1B 4J6, Telephone (709) 729-4729, Facsimile (709) 729-0654

Figgy Duff (Molasses Pudding)

**Beaton Tulk, MHA, Bonavista North, Newfoundland and Labrador,
Deputy Premier, Minister of Industry, Trade and Rural Development**

1 1/2 cups dried bread crumbs
1/3 cup all-purpose flour
3/4 cup raisins, soaked in 3 tablespoons of rum until plump, drained
1/4 teaspoon ground allspice
1/4 teaspoon ground cinnamon
1/4 teaspoon nutmeg
1/2 teaspoon baking powder
1/2 cup dark molasses
5 tablespoons melted butter
3 tablespoons dark rum
Maple syrup to taste
1 cup whipped cream
Strawberries, sliced, or other seasonal fruit

In a large mixing bowl, combine the bread crumbs, flour, soaked raisins, spices, baking powder, molasses, butter and rum.

Transfer the mixture to a plastic bag and wrap the bag in a double thickness of cotton cheesecloth. Tie the bag securely at the top.

In a large pot bring 6-8 cups of water to a boil and add the wrapped pudding. Cover and simmer over low heat for 1 1/2 hours. Remove the pudding from the water and drain. Cool for 20 minutes. Unwrap the pudding and transfer it to a cutting board.

Slice the pudding into 6 wedges. Drizzle maple syrup on each plate and place a wedge of pudding on the syrup. Place a dollop of whipped cream near to the pudding and garnish the whipped cream with sliced strawberries or your favourite fresh fruit.

"VERY MOLASSES-FLAVOURED AND QUITE HEAVY. DEFINITELY A SMALL-PORTION DESSERT."

– (TESTER) JULIANNE BEAUCHAMP, MUSIC EDUCATOR.

Notes:

"... a recipe that I often prepare for my family and friends."

Prince Edward Island
Legislative Assembly

Government Members' Office
PO Box 338
Charlottetown
Prince Edward Island
Canada C1A 7K7

Tel 902 368 4360
Fax 902 368 4377
www.gov.pe.ca/

Île-du-Prince-Édouard
Assemblée législative

Bureau des députés provinciaux
C.P. 338
Charlottetown
Île-du-Prince-Édouard
Canada C1A 7K7

Tél. : 902 368 4360
Téléc. : 902 368 4377
www.gov.pe.ca/

March 30, 2001

Ms. Yasmine John-Thorpe
150 Adamson Court
Penticton, BC V2A 7R8

Dear Ms. John-Thorpe:

Thank you for requesting a favourite recipe of mine to include in your cookbook.

One of my favourite recipe is Pineapple Whip and it is so simple to make. In our house it always goes over in a big way at mealtime. Although the whipping cream is a little heavy, this is a great recipe for a special treat every once in a while.

I hope you enjoy much success with your cookbook, "Taking the Heat: Canadian Politicians in the Kitchen."

Sincerely,

Jim Bagnall, MLA
District 4
Montague - Kilmuir

aah
Enclosure

Pineapple Whip

Jim Bagnall, MLA, Montague-Kilmuir, Prince Edward Island

2 packages Knox gelatin
1 19-ounce can crushed pineapple
Water and juice from pineapple to make 2 cups of liquid
1/2 cup white sugar

Notes:

Put above ingredients in saucepan and bring to a boil. Remove from heat. When mixture cools, put in fridge until it jells.

Add 1/2 pint whipped cream.

Keep dessert in fridge and let set until ready to serve.

"Very easy and tasty. Layered pineapple slices with red cherries in centre, poured in whipped mixture. Turned upside down – very attractive. Excellent as a dessert or side dish with ham or turkey."

– (Tester) Lorraine Pattison, writer.

"A well balanced life includes the preparation of wholesome, tasty meals. Eat well, but not too often, and energy is yours for the taking."

Prince Edward Island

Legislative Assembly

Government Members' Office
PO Box 338
Charlottetown
Prince Edward Island
Canada C1A 7K7

Tel 902 368 4360
Fax 902 368 4377
www.gov.pe.ca/

Île-du-Prince-Édouard

Assemblée législative

Bureau des députés provinciaux
C.P. 338
Charlottetown
Île-du-Prince-Édouard
Canada C1A 7K7

Tél. : 902 368 4360
Téléc. : 902 368 4377
www.gov.pe.ca/

PARVA SUB INGENTI

March 30, 2001

Ms. Yasmine John-Thorpe
150 Adamson Court
Penticton, BC V2A 7R8

Dear Ms. John-Thorpe:

Thanks for your request to submit my favourite recipe for inclusion in your cookbook.

My favourite recipe of Traditional Cheese Cake is really an easy recipe to prepare and we never have any disappointed faces when it is presented at the table in our home. Everyone will enjoy this quick and simple recipe.

Please be assured of my best wishes for the success of your cookbook, "Taking the Heat: Canadian Politicians in the Kitchen."

Sincerely,

Jamie Ballem

Hon. Jamie Ballem,
Minister, Health and Social Services

aah
Enclosure

Traditional Cheese Cake

Jamie Ballem, MLA, Stanhope-East Royalty, Prince Edward Island, Minister of Health and Social Services

Base:

2 cups graham wafer crumbs
1/2 cup butter or margarine
2 tablespoons white sugar

Mix crumbs, butter and sugar. Press into 9"x9" pan and bake for 15 minutes at 375°F.

Filling:

1 8-ounce package cream cheese
1 cup icing sugar
1 package Dream Whip or 2 cups whipped cream

Mix cream cheese and sugar. Fold in prepared Dream Whip or whipping cream and spread mixture on wafer bottom. Top with canned cherry filling.

"EASY AND STRAIGHTFORWARD. I MADE IN A PIE DISH – RESERVING 1/2 THE GRAHAM MIXTURE TO USE AS TOPPING. USED 2 CUPS WHIPPING CREAM AND MADE A DAY AHEAD."

– (TESTER) YASMIN JOHN-THORPE, WRITER AND COOKBOOK COMPILER.

Notes:

"The secret to cooking is to always use the best ingredients. For example, I always use only real butter. I find in baking, as in life, what you put into it, determines the end result."

Prince Edward Island | **Île-du-Prince-Édouard**

Legislative Assembly

Assemblée législative

Government Members' Office
PO Box 338
Charlottetown
Prince Edward Island
Canada C1A 7K7

Bureau des députés provinciaux
C.P. 338
Charlottetown
Île-du-Prince-Édouard
Canada C1A 7K7

Tel 902 368 4360
Fax 902 368 4377
www.gov.pe.ca/

Tél. : 902 368 4360
Téléc. : 902 368 4377
www.gov.pe.ca/

March 30, 2001

Ms. Yasmine John-Thorpe
150 Adamson Court
Penticton, BC V2A 7R8

Dear Ms. John-Thorpe:

Thank you for requesting a favourite recipe from me to include in your cookbook.

My favourite recipe, Daisy's Pudding Cake, is so simple to make and everyone who tries it loves it. You will note any kind of berries can be use in it, but being a Tory I always choose "blue"berries! I'm sure everyone will enjoy it as much as our family does.

Here's hoping you have great success with your cookbook, "Taking the Heat: Canadian Politicians in the Kitchen."

Sincerely,

Hon. Greg Deighan,
Minister, Tourism

aah
Enclosure

Daisy's Pudding Cake

Greg Deighan, MLA, Wilmot-Summerside, Prince Edward Island, Minister of Tourism

2 cups blueberries
1 cup all-purpose flour
1 teaspoon baking powder
1/4 teaspoon salt
3 tablespoons melted shortening (or 1/4 cup vegetable oil)
3/4 cup sugar
1/2 cup milk
1 cup sugar
1 tablespoon cornstarch
1 cup boiling water

Notes:

Place berries in bottom of 8" x 8" pan. Mix together flour, baking powder, salt, shortening, 3/4 cup sugar and milk. Spread over berries. Mix cornstarch and 1 cup sugar and sprinkle over the batter in pan. Pour 1 cup boiling water over top and bake at 350°F for 45 minutes. Serve hot or cold with pouring cream, whipped cream or ice cream.

Suggestion: Raspberries, strawberries, rhubarb or apple can be substituted for blueberries.

"QUICK TO PUT TOGETHER. ALSO WORKS WITH FROZEN BLUEBERRIES. DESSERT LIKE GRANDMA USED TO MAKE."

– (TESTER) CAROLEE FINCH, OFFICE MANAGER/ BOOKKEEPER AND OUTDOORS ENTHUSIAST.

"Follow directions and always read the black print."

Prince Edward Island — Île-du-Prince-Édouard

Legislative Assembly — Assemblée législative

Government Members' Office
PO Box 338
Charlottetown
Prince Edward Island
Canada C1A 7K7

Bureau des députés provinciaux
C.P. 338
Charlottetown
Île-du-Prince-Édouard
Canada C1A 7K7

Tel 902 368 4360
Fax 902 368 4377
www.gov.pe.ca/

Tél. : 902 368 4360
Téléc. : 902 368 4377
www.gov.pe.ca/

March 30, 2001

Ms. Yasmine John-Thorpe
150 Adamson Court
Penticton, BC V2A 7R8

Dear Ms. John-Thorpe:

Your request for a favourite recipe arrived on my desk a short time ago.

This Cream Cheese Fruit Cake is great anytime, not just at Christmas when we traditionally think of having fruit cake. It is quick and simple to make and I can attest to the fact that it is delicious. I'm sure everyone will enjoy this recipe.

Here's wishing you much success with your cookbook, "Taking the Heat: Canadian Politicians in the Kitchen."

Sincerely,

Hon. Chester Gillan, Minister
Fisheries, Aquaculture & Environment

aah
Enclosure

Cream Cheese Fruit Cake

Chester Gillan, MLA, Parkdale-Belverdere, Prince Edward Island, Minister Fisheries, Aquaculture and Environment

1 cup butter
1 1/2 cups white sugar
4 eggs
1 8–ounce package cream cheese
1 1/2 teaspoons vanilla
2 cups flour
1/2 pound cherries (glazed)
1 pound raisins
1 1/2 teaspoon baking powder
1 small package slivered almonds

Cream butter, sugar and cream cheese. Add eggs individually. Add vanilla. Reserve 1/4 cup flour for the fruit. Add flour and baking powder to cream cheese mixture, then add fruit.

Line tube pan with wax paper.

Bake at 325°F for 1 hour and 20 minutes.

"FLAVOURFUL, SOMEWHAT BISCUIT-LIKE IN TEXTURE. NOT AS MOIST AS TRADITIONAL FRUIT CAKE."

– (TESTER) JULIANNE BEAUCHAMP, MUSIC EDUCATOR.

Notes:

"This Cream Cheese Fruit Cake is great any time, not just at Christmas when we traditionally think of having fruit cake. It is quick and simple to make and I can attest to the fact that it is delicious. I'm sure everyone will enjoy this recipe."

Prince Edward Island
Legislative Assembly

Government Members' Office
PO Box 338
Charlottetown
Prince Edward Island
Canada C1A 7K7

Île-du-Prince-Édouard
Assemblée législative

Bureau des députés provinciaux
C.P. 338
Charlottetown
Île-du-Prince-Édouard
Canada C1A 7K7

Tél. : 902 368 4360
Téléc. : 902 368 4377
www.gov.pe.ca/

PARVA SUB INGENTI

Tel 902 368 4360
Fax 902 368 4377
www.gov.pe.ca/

March 30, 2001

Ms. Yasmine John-Thorpe
150 Adamson Court
Penticton, BC V2A 7R8

Dear Ms. John-Thorpe:

A Canadian political cookbook is such a great idea!

As you will note, my recipe for "Election Cake" includes something sweet, something tart, a little promise, and a whole lot of nuts – the perfect recipe for any politician! I hope everyone who tries it will enjoy it as much as I do.

All my best wishes for success in your efforts with "Taking the Heat: Canadian Politicians in the Kitchen."

Sincerely,

Wes MacAleer

Wes MacAleer, MLA
District 14
Charlottetown - Spring Park

aah
Enclosure

Election Cake

Wes MacAleer, MLA, Charlottetown–Spring Park, Prince Edward Island, Minister Community Services & Attorney General

1 orange
Thin outer rind of one orange
2 cups flour
1 teaspoon baking soda
1 teaspoon salt
1 cup walnuts
2 eggs
1/2 cup sour cream
1/2 cup brandy
1/2 cup shortening
1 cup sugar
1 cup raisins
Topping:
Juice from orange
1/2 cup sugar

Heat oven to 350°F. Grease and flour a 9" x 13" cake pan. Squeeze orange and set juice aside for topping. Sift flour, baking soda and salt into large mixer bowl. Blender-chop nuts and add to flour mixture. Put eggs, cream, brandy, butter and sugar into blender container, cover and process at #10 until smooth and well blended. Stop blender and add orange rind and raisins. Cover and process at #10 until raisins are finely chopped. Add to flour mixture and mix at #3 until well mixed. Pour into prepared cake pan and bake 30–35 minutes.

While cake is baking, mix topping ingredients. As soon as cake is removed from oven, poke holes throughout top with skewer and pour topping over. When cool, frost with butter cream icing. Makes 15–18 servings.

"Directions very easy to follow. Batter has to be spread in the cake pan as there is not a lot of it. However, it rises beautifully while baking. I baked in a preheated oven for 30 minutes."

– (Tester) Yasmin John-Thorpe, writer and cookbook compiler.

"Very moist with a great orange flavour."

– (Taster) Sue Reid, teacher.

Notes:

"As you will note, my recipe for 'Election Cake' includes something sweet, something tart, a little promise and a whole lot of nuts – the perfect recipe for any politician! I hope everyone who tries it will enjoy it as much as I do."

Prince Edward Island
Legislative Assembly

Government Members' Office
PO Box 338
Charlottetown
Prince Edward Island
Canada C1A 7K7

Tel 902 368 4360
Fax 902 368 4377
www.gov.pe.ca/

Île-du-Prince-Édouard
Assemblée législative

Bureau des députés provinciaux
C.P. 338
Charlottetown
Île-du-Prince-Édouard
Canada C1A 7K7

Tél. : 902 368 4360
Téléc. : 902 368 4377
www.gov.pe.ca/

March 30, 2001

Ms. Yasmine John-Thorpe
150 Adamson Court
Penticton, BC V2A 7R8

Dear Ms. John-Thorpe:

Your request for a favourite recipe was received by my office a short while ago.

This recipe for Chocolate Chip Cookies comes from a cookbook prepared by my children when they were grade one students and they enjoyed helping make them. We had a grand time in the kitchen working together! The recipe is simple, quick, and easy and everyone loves them. My children are now 19, 18, and 15 and are now well able to make the cookies for themselves.

I hope everyone who tries the recipe enjoys it and I truly wish you much success with "Taking the Heat: Canadian Politicians in the Kitchen."

Sincerely,

Beth MacKenzie

Beth MacKenzie, MLA
District 18
Park Corner - Oyster Bed

aah
Enclosure

C:\WINNT\Profiles\aahennessey\Beth-cookbook.wpd

Chocolate Chip Cookies

Beth MacKenzie, MLA, Park Corner-Oyster Bed, Prince Edward Island

2/3 cup butter
2/3 cup shortening
1 cup brown sugar
1 cup white sugar
2 eggs
2 teaspoons vanilla
2 1/2 cups flour
1 teaspoon baking soda

Blend well. Stir in 500 gram bag of chocolate chips. Drop from teaspoon onto greased cookie sheet. Bake at 375°F for 8-10 minutes.

"THESE WERE EXCELLENT. MY KIDS LOVED THEM."
– (TESTER) CHRISTINE COCKER, ASSISTANT STORE MANAGER.

Notes:

"As a politician I attend many luncheons, dinners and evening socials. My husband loves to accompany me because he's then assured of a hot meal, served with a smile."

Prince Edward Island — Île-du-Prince-Édouard

Legislative Assembly — Assemblée législative

Government Members' Office
PO Box 338
Charlottetown
Prince Edward Island
Canada C1A 7K7

Bureau des députés provinciaux
C.P. 338
Charlottetown
Île-du-Prince-Édouard
Canada C1A 7K7

Tel 902 368 4360
Fax 902 368 4377
www.gov.pe.ca/

Tél. : 902 368 4360
Téléc. : 902 368 4377
www.gov.pe.ca/

March 30, 2001

Ms. Yasmine John-Thorpe
150 Adamson Court
Penticton, BC V2A 7R8

Dear Ms. John-Thorpe:

Your request for my favourite recipe arrived in my office a few days ago.

My favourite recipe is one my Mom has made for the family for many years. This recipe for Saucy Minty Mocha Pudding is just great and everyone who makes it will have trouble keeping little fingers out of the bowl as it is being prepared – big fingers too!

I am sure you will have much success with your cookbook, "Taking the Heat: Canadian Politicians in the Kitchen."

Sincerely,

Andy Mooney

Andy Mooney, MLA
District 1
Souris - Elmira

aah
Enclosure

Saucy Minty Mocha Pudding

Andy Mooney, MLA, Souris–Elmira, Prince Edward Island, Deputy Speaker

Combine:

1/4 cup cocoa
1/2 cup granulated sugar
1/2 cup lightly packed brown sugar

Gradually stir in 2 cups of hot coffee and a few drops of peppermint flavouring. Keep mixture simmering hot.

Cake Batter:

1/3 cup shortening
2/3 cup white sugar
1 egg
1/2 teaspoon vanilla

Beat until fluffy. Add:

1 teaspoon vanilla

Blend:

1 cup flour
1 1/2 teaspoons baking powder
1/4 teaspoon salt

Add to creamed mixture alternately with 1/3 cup milk. Combine well. Turn onto a greased 8" pan and pour coffee mixture over cake. Do not stir. Bake in preheated 350°F oven for 45–50 minutes. Serve warm.

"Very easy to prepare. I recommend using 1 cup of coffee as pudding is very moist. Very tasty. A must for the coffee drinker's palette. The flavours dance together, making this a cuddle food for those chilly nights by the fire, or on a twilight porch."

– (Tester) Karen Mathieson, writer and student.

Notes:

"Eat, drink and be merry, but get the crop in first."

Judy Junor, MLA

Saskatoon Eastview
#1 - 3012 Louise Street
Saskatoon, SK S7J 3L8
Phone: (306) 477-4233
Fax (306) 477-4236

Regina Office
Room 203
Legislative Building
Regina, SK S4S 0B3
Phone: (306) 787-0901

March 27, 2000

Yasmin John-Thorpe
150 Adamson Court
Penticton, BC V2A 7R8

Dear Yasmin,

Well, here it is finally. It took me awhile to find a quote that Judy was happy with but I think she picked a good one. I do not have a photo of Judy preparing the dish. Sorry.

The quote is quite serious and was said by Tommy Douglas:

"Never be afraid of something because it is new…Never discard something just because it is old…Measure your life not by what you get but by what you give."

I think your project is very exciting and I wish you all the best with it. If you have time, please let me know when it will hit the book stands and I'll be sure to purchase a copy.

All the best!

April F. Anderson
Constituency Assistant for
Saskatoon Eastview

Mexican Chocolate Cake

Judy Junor, MLA, Saskatoon Eastview, Saskatchewan

1/2 cup margarine
1/2 cup oil
2 squares unsweetened chocolate
2 cups flour
1 teaspoon baking soda
2 cups sugar
1/2 cup sour milk
2 eggs, beaten
1 teaspoon cinnamon
1 teaspoon vanilla
1 cup water

Notes:

Combine 1/2 cup margarine, 1/2 cup oil, 2 squares unsweetened chocolate and 1 cup water and heat until chocolate is melted. Combine remaining ingredients and then add melted chocolate mixture. Beat until mixed. Pour into greased pan (9" x 13"). Bake 40–50 minutes at 350°F.

"I USED A BUNDT PAN AND IT CAME OUT BEAUTIFUL."

– (TESTER) JULIANNE BEAUCHAMP, MUSIC EDUCATOR.

"Never be afraid of something because it is new... Never discard something just because it is old... Measure your life not by what you get but by what you give." – Tommy Douglas

Hon. Jim Melenchuk, MLA
Saskatoon Northwest Constituency
#3 415 – 51st St. E.
Saskatoon SK S7K 6V4

Saskatchewan Legislative Assembly

Member

March 23, 2000

Yasmsin John-Thorpe
150 Adamson Court
Penticton, British Columbia
V2A 7R8

Dear Mr. Yasmin John-Thorpe:

Enclosed please find one of my favourite recipes together with a photo and a quote as per your request.

Good luck with your manuscript.

Sincerely yours,

Hon. Jim Melenchuk MLA
Saskatoon Northwest Constituency
Minister of Education

JWM/vm

Recyclable Paper

Jim's No Bake Chocolate Cheesecake

Jim Melenchuk, MLA, Saskatoon Northwest, Saskatchewan, Minister of Education

1/3 cup chopped almonds
2 packages cream cheese
1 cup white sugar
6 squares semi-sweet chocolate
1/4 cup cold water
1 envelope unflavoured gelatin
1 cup whipping cream

Notes:

Pre preparation:

Toast almonds. Soften the cream cheese. Melt and cool the chocolate. Whip the whipping cream.

Grease an 8 1/2″ spring form pan. Sprinkle with the almonds. In a separate bowl beat the cream cheese until smooth. Add the sugar and chocolate and blend together. Put cold water in small saucepan and sprinkle the gelatin over the top. Let stand for 5 minutes and then stir over low heat until the gelatin dissolves. Pour the warm gelatin into the cream cheese and stir. Then blend the cream cheese mixture into the whipped cream. Pour into pan and chill for 3 hours minimum. You may decorate the cheesecake with melted chocolate or additional almonds if you like.

"I made this dessert for the neighbourhood 'progressive supper' group. It is easy to make and tastes delicious."

"So simple even our dishwasher could have prepared it."

– (Tester) Mike Large, chef Gun Barrel Grill Restaurant.

"Creamy texture with incredible taste. Plated beautifully."

– (Taster) Roberta Robertson, Interior Decorator and Chef.

PREMIER OF SASKATCHEWAN

LEGISLATIVE BUILDING
REGINA, CANADA S4S 0B3

1149/2000

February 14, 2000

Yasmin John-Thorpe
150 Adamson Court
PENTICTON BC V2A 7R8

Dear Ms. John-Thorpe:

Thank you for your letter regarding plans for a cookbook called *Taking the Heat: Canadian Politicians in the Kitchen*. I am pleased to provide you with a recipe for a family favourite, Ukrainian Walnut Torte, for use in your cookbook.

Please accept my best wishes for success with this interesting project.

Yours sincerely,

Roy Romanow

Roy Romanow
Premier

Enclosure

Internet e-mail: premier@gov.sk.ca

pcu-regina

Ukrainian Walnut Torte

Roy Romanow, Former MLA, Saskatoon Riversdale, Former Premier of Saskatchewan

12 eggs (set aside 2 yolks for filling)
1 cup white sugar
1 cup ground walnuts
4 tablespoons flour
1 teaspoon baking powder

Filling:
1/2 cup butter, unsalted
1 cup icing sugar
2 egg yolks
5 teaspoons instant coffee
2 tablespoons sugar
2 tablespoons water

Notes:

Beat 10 yolks with sugar until fluffy. Combine walnuts, flour and baking powder. Next beat 12 egg whites until stiff and add to first mixture. Bake at 350°F for 50 minutes. Set aside to cool.

Next, prepare the filling. Cream butter and icing sugar and 2 egg yolks; set aside and mix instant coffee, 2 tablespoons sugar and water. Boil for a few minutes, cool and add to the butter mixture. To make cream filling, cut cooled cake into 3 layers and fill.

"I SUGGEST THE FILLING FOR THE RECIPE BE DOUBLED AS THE RESTAURANT STAFF ENJOYED THE TASTE OF THIS TORTE, BUT FELT THERE WAS NOT ENOUGH FILLING."

– (TESTER) RALPH H. KORDASS C.C.C., HEAD CHEF MAGNUM'S ON THE LAKE RESTAURANT, LAKESIDE RESORT AND CASINO.

"I am pleased to provide you with a recipe for a family favourite, Ukranian Walnut Torte..."

Yukon Legislative Assembly

Box 2703, Whitehorse, Yukon Y1A 2C6

June 27, 2000

Yasmin John-Thorpe
150 Adamson Court
Penticton, British Columbia
V2A 7R8

Dear Yasmin John-Thorpe:

Enclosed you will find Sue Edelman's photograph. As this photo came from Sue's personal files we appreciate its prompt return when you are finished using it.

You can find out more information about Sue on this website - www.gov.yk.ca/leg-assembly/mlas. Although the information from this website contains Sue's ministry responsibilities the cookbook is something she supports on her own as a member of the Yukon Liberal Caucus in her position as MLA for Riverdale South. It is important that her MLA status only, is associated with the cookbook.

Sue is very grateful that you are providing her with a copy of the cookbook and anticipates its distribution. Please feel welcome to contact the office at any time. 867-667-8881 Email: Sue.Edelman@gov.yk.ca

Sincerely,

Christine Smith
Assistant to Sue Edelman

Stove Top Cookies

Sue Edelman, MLA, Riverdale South, Yukon, Yukon Liberal Caucus

2 cups sugar
1/2 cup cocoa
1/2 cup milk
1/2 cup butter
1 teaspoon vanilla
3 cups rolled oats (instant)
1 cup coconut

Notes:

Cook first 4 ingredients over medium heat till it boils, remove from heat and add vanilla, oats and coconut. Drop onto wax paper by the teaspoon for company or by the tablespoon for family!

"VERY QUICK AND EASY. ONE OF MY FAMILY'S FAVOURITES."

– (TESTER) CAROLEE FINCH, OFFICE MANAGER/ BOOKKEEPER AND OUTDOORS ENTHUSIAST.

"This was my favourite recipe as a child–now I share this with my children."

Chocolate Inside Out Bundt Cake

Doreen E. Hamilton, MLA, Regina Wascana Plains, Saskatchewan

1 Duncan Hines Cake Mix
1 package instant chocolate pudding
2 eggs
1 3/4 cups of milk
12 ounces chocolate chips

Preheat oven to 350°F. Spray Bundt pan. Beat above items for 4 minutes. Stir in 12 ounces of chocolate chips. Bake 50–55 minutes. Let sit in pan for 15–20 minutes before inverting.

"Very easy to make. Tasty and chocolate-flavoured. I made at Christmas time, putting in an Xmas Tree pan. I iced with fluffy icing tinted green (1 envelope Dream Whip, 1 pkg. instant vanilla pudding) and 1 1/2 cups cold milk. Beat until stiff, add green colour, frost and chill."

– (Tester) Lorraine Pattison, writer.

Mary Hodder's Company's Coming White Raisin Pudding

Mary Hodder, MHA, Burin–Placentia West, Newfoundland and Labrador, Deputy Chair of Committees

2 1/2 cups white flour
2 tablespoons sugar
1 teaspoon salt
3 teaspoons baking powder
1/4 cup margarine
1 package raisins or 2 1/2 cup blueberries

Mix above ingredients with 1 cup of cold water and spoon into a well greased mould. Fill 2/3 full and cover with greased tight-fitting lid. Place in a pot that is 2/3 full of boiling water, replacing water as needed. Boil for approximately 1 1/2 hours. Remove from mould and serve with vanilla sauce.

Vanilla Sauce

1/4 cup butter or margarine
1 teaspoon flour
1 teaspoon vanilla
1 cup milk
1/2 cup white sugar
1/4 cup coconut rum

Melt butter, add flour, dash of salt and vanilla. Add milk and sugar. Continue cooking over medium heat until thickened, stirring constantly. Serve hot over pudding.

"Use small package raisins (2 cups) and add another 1/2 cup water to mixture. The coconut rum used in the sauce is on the expensive side. Easy to make if you have a covered pudding mold."

– (Tester) Adelaide Lopes, health care worker.

Irish Cream Cake

Bob Mills, MP, Red Deer, Alberta

1 box (18.25 ounces) yellow cake mix
1 package (4 ounces) instant chocolate pudding
3/4 cup corn oil
1/4 cup water
1/4 cup vodka
1/4 cup Irish Cream liqueur
4 eggs

Combine all ingredients in large bowl. Beat until smooth. Bake in greased and floured bundt or angel food cake pan at 350°F for 45 minutes. Cool on rack for 25 minutes. Turn out on cake dish and serve with vanilla ice cream.

"Very easy to make. Extra thick batter makes it hard to beat. It took 50 mins. to bake. I used a butter icing with Bacardi dark chocolate rum liqueur. The cake has a very tasty flavour – will use for company."

– (Tester) Lorraine Pattison, writer.

Chocolate Dream Squares

Bob Mills, MP, Red Deer, Alberta

20 crushed graham crackers mixed with 2 tablespoons butter
2 sticks butter
2 cups confectioners' sugar
3 eggs
3 squares chocolate, melted
1 teaspoon vanilla
1/2 cup crushed walnuts (optional)

Line 8" square pan with half of graham cracker mixture (press down). With electric mixer cream butter, add 2 cups of confectioners' sugar; add eggs one at a time, blending well; add melted chocolate (Chocobake may be used) and 1 teaspoon vanilla. Spread mixture over crumbs. Sprinkle reserved crumb mixture over all; optional nuts may be spread over top. Refrigerate until firm, about 4 hours.

A very rich dessert – may be served with whipped cream. Can be frozen ahead and defrosted in refrigerator for 3–4 hours.

"Easy and fast to make. Very rich with a subtle taste."

– (Tester) Alan E. Longworth, writer.

Christmas Pie

Wes MacAleer, MLA, Charlottetown–Spring Park, Prince Edward Island, Minister Community Services & Attorney General

Pastry for single pie crust
2 egg whites
1/4 cup sugar for meringue
1/2 cup sugar for filling
1/2 teaspoon vanilla
1/2 teaspoon cream of tartar
3 tablespoons cornstarch
3 cups frozen strawberries
Sliced kiwis
1 cup whipping cream

Prepare and roll out pastry. Line a 9" pie plate. Trim to 1/2" beyond edge. Flute and prick pastry. Bake for 10–12 minutes at 450°F. Cool.

For meringue, beat egg whites, vanilla and cream of tartar until soft peaks form. Gradually add 1/4 cup sugar, continuing beating until stiff peaks form. Spread on the bottom and sides of pastry. Bake for 12 minutes at 350°F. Cool.

Mash berries, adding water to measure 2 cups. Combine 1/2 cup sugar and cornstarch, add to mashed berries. Cook over medium heat until bubbly, stirring often. Cook and stir 2 minutes more. Cool. Spread over meringue. Chill. Whip cream and spread over pie. Top with sliced kiwis. Enjoy!

Hint: If making a day ahead, stabilize whipped cream with 1 package "Whip It".

"This is a wonderful dessert to serve on a Christmas buffet or as your dinner's grand finale."
– Wes MacAleer

"VERY UNUSUAL WITH HAVING A CRUST THEN MERINGUE AND THEN THE FILLING. VERY LIGHT AND REFRESHING. WOULD BE SUITABLE FOR A SUMMER DESSERT. EXCELLENT COLOUR.

– (TESTER) JANELLE BREESE-BIAGIONI, AUTHOR.

Creamy Lemon Pie

Elinor Caplan, MP, Thornhill, Ontario, Minister of Citizenship and Immigration

3 9–inch pie shells
4 cups (2 pints) whipping cream
1 10–ounce tin condensed milk
1 6–ounce can frozen concentrated lemonade (not pink)

Bake pie shells and cool. Whip cream with hand mixer in a large bowl. Add thawed lemonade and condensed milk. Blend well. Pour into shells and chill. Freezes well.

"THIS WAS TOO EASY TO MAKE. I FELT GUILTY SERVING IT TO DINNER GUESTS."

– (TESTER) YASMIN JOHN-THORPE, WRITER AND COOKBOOK COMPILER.

"VERY GOOD, CREAMY TEXTURE AND A LIGHT REFRESHING FLAVOUR. YUM!"

– (TASTER) ANN GREGOIRE, FEDERAL CIVIL SERVANT

MORE...

ALBERTA
CHILDREN'S SERVICES

Office of the Minister

August 22, 2000

Ms. Yasmin John-Thorpe
150 Adamson Court
Penticton, British Columbia
V2A 7R8

Dear Ms. John-Thorpe:

Re: TAKING THE HEAT: Canadian Politicians in the Kitchen

In response to your recent request for material for your innovative cookbook, I provide the following:

Recipe: Beating the Heat

2 quarts fresh squeezed limes
1 cup packed fresh mint leaves
2 cups sugar (to taste)
Mix in blender

Mix one part of this syrup with approximately five parts of sparkling water and serve. (This drink is a wonderful and refreshing treat!)

Quote: "Never get off your horse to fight with the pigs." ..... an oldie but goodie!

I would really appreciate receiving a copy of this unique cookbook. Thank you for the opportunity to participate.

Sincerely yours,

Iris Evans
Minister

Enclosure

107 Legislature Building, Edmonton, Alberta, Canada T5K 2B6 Telephone 780/415-4890, Fax 780/415-4859

Printed on recycled paper

Beating the Heat

Iris Evans, MLA, Sherwood Park, Alberta, Minister Children's Services

2 quarts fresh squeezed limes
1 cup packed fresh mint leaves
2 cups sugar (to taste)

Mix one part of this syrup with approximately five parts of sparking water and serve. (This drink is a wonderful and refreshing treat!)

"I USED THE JUICE OF 12 MEDIUM LARGE LIMES AND BLENDED ALL INGREDIENTS UNTIL MINT LEAVES WERE ABSORBED INTO THE LIQUID. I FILLED 1/4 OF A GLASS WITH THE SYRUP, AND TOPPED IT OFF WITH GINGER ALE AND CRUSHED ICE. THIS IS VERY, VERY DELICIOUS."

– (TESTER) THORA PAUL, RETIRED CORPORATE EXECUTIVE AND FLORIDA RESIDENT

Notes:

"Never get off your horse to fight with the pigs.".... an oldie but a goodie!

Province of
British Columbia
Legislative Assembly

OFFICE OF THE OFFICIAL OPPOSITION OF BRITISH COLUMBIA

Bill Barisoff, M.L.A.
(Okanagan-Boundary)

Constituency Office: 34853 — 97th Street (Box 1768), Oliver, B.C. V0H 1T0
Telephone: (250) 498-3001 Fax: (250) 498-3638

Room 201, Parliament Buildings, Victoria, B.C. V8V 1X4
Telephone: (250) 387-2814 Fax: (250) 387-2759
e-mail: Barisoff@cablelan.net

PEROGIES

Submitted by Ida Barisoff

2 eggs
2 cups milk
1 tsp. salt
2 cups oil (generous)
2 tbsp baking powder
Add enough flour to make a light dough (about 5 ½ cups)

FILLING:

Using dry cottage cheese, freeze it in a carton. Take out of freezer and once thawed, squeeze out all of the moisture. Add an egg and a pinch of salt.

Roll out dough and cut into squares approx. 2 ½" x 2 ½". Spoon a bit of filling into the perogie and seal edges.

In a pot of boiling water, add a drop of oil and a pinch of salt. Drop perogies in the water and cook until they start to float. Drain in a collander and serve with sour cream, bacon bits, cheese etc.

Bill Barisoff

Perogies

Bill Barisoff, MLA, Okanagan-Penticton, British Columbia, Minister of Revenue

2 eggs
2 cups milk
1 tsp. salt
2 cups oil (generous)
2 tbsp. baking powder

Notes:

Add enough flour to make a light dough (about 5 1/2 cups).

Filling:

Using dry cottage cheese, freeze it in a carton. Take out of freezer and, once thawed, squeeze out all of the moisture. Add an egg and a pinch of salt.

Roll out dough and cut into squares approx. 2 1/2" x 2 1/2". Spoon a bit of filling into the perogie and seal edges.

In a pot of boiling water, add a drop of oil and a pinch of salt. Drop perogies in the water and cook until they start to float. Drain in a colander and serve with sour cream, bacon bits, cheese, etc.

"VERY EASY TO MAKE; A TOTAL OF 10 MINUTES TO MAKE THE RECIPE. I USED LESS THAN 2 CUPS OF OIL. THE DOUGH WAS VERY EASY TO HANDLE. I RECOMMEND A 750 ML. DRY COTTAGE CHEESE AS THE RECIPE DIDN'T SPECIFY THE AMOUNT. THESE PEROGIES WERE VERY TASTY WITH ONIONS, SOUR CREAM AND MY FAVOURITE, SALSA."

– (TESTER) SUSAN MATHIESON, PACKER, CANWOOD PINE FURNITURE FACTORY, PENTICTON

My Mom's (Ida Barisoff) favourite perogies recipe.

Chai Tea

preparation time: 20 min
cooking time: 10 min

This recipe serves 4 people

Ingredients:

3 cups milk
3 cups spring water
1/3 cups sugar
2 tablespoons black tea leaves
1 (2-inch) cinnamon stick
8 whole black peppercorns
4 whole cloves
8 cardamom seeds
1/4 teaspoons cumin seeds
4 whole allspice berries
1/4 teaspoon fresh grated nutmeg

Directions:

Bring the milk, water, sugar, and black tea to a boil in a heavy saucepan. Remove the pan from the heat, add the spices, and let steep, covered, for 15 minutes. Return the mixture to high heat, and just when the mixture boils, strain it into a teapot or individual teacups. Serve immediately or store, covered, in the refrigerator, and reheat to serve.

Chai (Tea)

Ujjal Dosanjh, Former MLA, Vancouver–Kensington, Former Premier of British Columbia

3 cups milk
3 cups spring water
1/3 cup sugar
2 tablespoons black tea leaves
1 2" cinnamon stick
8 whole black peppercorns
4 whole cloves
8 cardamom seeds
1/4 teaspoon cumin seeds
4 whole allspice berries
1/4 teaspoon fresh grated nutmeg

Notes:

Bring the milk, water, sugar and black tea to a boil in a heavy saucepan. Remove the pan from the heat, add the spices and let steep, covered, for 15 minutes. Return the mixture to high heat and, just when the mixture boils, strain it into a teapot or individual teacups. Serve immediately or store, covered, in the refrigerator and reheat to serve.

"I used the ingredients to make Chai tea latté and it is excellent. Ingredients are quite expensive though. Careful, it boils over very easily."

– (Tester) Maureen McDonald, sports enthusiast and adventure traveller.

"Civility and respect are gained by understanding a fundamental truth in our parliamentary democracy: that political opponents are rivals, not enemies."

GOVERNMENT HOUSE
1401 ROCKLAND AVENUE
VICTORIA, BRITISH COLUMBIA
V8S 1V9

May 29, 2000

<u>Personal</u>
Mrs. Yasmin Thorpe
150 Adamson Court
Penticton, British Columbia
V2A 7R8

Dear Mrs. Thorpe:

It was a great pleasure to have met you, and Mrs. Gardom and I much enjoyed our discussion.

You have certainly enjoyed an interesting life.

Many thanks for your book about Penticton – much appreciated.

Helen will mail you a recipe.

All the best.

Garde B. Gardom, Q.C.
Lieutenant-Governor

Pickled Peaches or Pears

Garde B. Gardom, Q.C., Lieutenant-Governor of British Columbia

8 pounds peaches or pears
4 pounds best brown sugar
1 quart vinegar
10 sticks cinnamon
1 teaspoon whole cloves, whole allspice, mixed pickling spice; tie all in cheesecloth bag

Combine vinegar, sugar and spices and boil for 10 minutes. Skim well. Add fruit and simmer for 10 minutes.

Next morning, pour off juice and boil 1 minute. Pour back on.

The following morning, pour off juice, and boil 5-10 minutes. Bottle in sterilized jars.

"I PICKED PEARS OFF MY TREE FOR THIS RECIPE. PEARS WERE LARGE SO I CUT THEM IN HALF. DURING COOKING, A LOVELY CHRISTMAS SMELL TRAVELLED ALL THROUGH THE HOUSE. WOULD MAKE AN ATTRACTIVE DISPLAY AROUND THE TURKEY AT CHRISTMAS. MAYBE NEXT TIME I'LL CHOOSE SMALLER PEARS AND LEAVE THEM WHOLE."

– (TESTER) ROBERTA ROBERTSON, INTERIOR DECORATOR AND CHEF.

Notes:

"It was a great pleasure to have met you, and Mrs. Gardom and I much enjoyed our discussion."

Rick Thorpe, M.L.A.
(Okanagan-Penticton)

Province of
British Columbia
Legislative Assembly

Constituency mailing address
Suite 103-74 Wade Avenue, East
Penticton, B.C. V2A 8M4
Phone: (250) 493-7111
Fax: (250) 493-7174
Email: rick.thorpe.mla@leg.bc.ca

Victoria mailing address
Parliament Buildings
Victoria, B.C. V8V 1X4
Phone: (250) 387-2493
Fax: (250) 387-2497

BRITISH COLUMBIA
TO DIE FOR VEGGIE LASAGNA by Rick Thorpe, MLA

1 box lasagna noodles
1 cup diced broccoli
1 cup diced carrots
1 cup diced califlower
1 cup diced zuccini
1 cup diced celery
1 cup diced onions
½ cup diced red pepper
½ cup diced yellow pepper
1 cup sliced mushrooms
3 cloves crushed garlic
½ cup olive oil

1 large sprig basil (chopped)
1 large sprig fresh thyme
1 large sprig fresh rosemary
1 large sprig fresh oregano (chopped)
1 large sprig fresh cilantro (chopped)
1 - 796 ml can chopped stewed tomatoes
1 - 398 ml can whole leaf spinach
(drain liquid and chop)
1 - 700 ml jar Classico pasta sauce
(my favorite: tomato and pesto)
2 cups grated sharp (old) cheddar cheese
2 cups grated mozzarella cheese
1 - 500 ml tub 2% cottage cheese

Over medium fire heat oil in large pot with lid. Add onion and garlic - fry for 2 minutes (stir often)
Add all diced and sliced veggies. Stir, reduce heat and cover.
Cook for 10 minutes, stirring occasionally.
Add spices, tomatoes, pasta sauce and chopped spinach. Bring to a boil - reducing heat.
Cover and cook for another 10 minutes - stirring to prevent sticking or burning.
Remove from heat and discard spice stalks from thyme and rosemary.
Assemble lasagna in a 13x9x2 inch dish.
Ladle a little veggie sauce in the bottom of the dish first.
Lay out noodles to cover dish bottom.
Ladle sauce over noodles and cover with ½ the cheddar cheese.
Repeat layer of noodles and sauce and cover with ½ the mozzarella cheese.
Repeat layer of noodles and sauce and cover with the tub of cottage cheese.
Repeat layer of noodles and sauce and cover with remainder of the cheddar cheese.
Top layer of noodles and sauce and cover with remainder of the mozzarella cheese.
Cover loosely with tin foil.
(Lasagna may be frozen at this time - defrost before baking)
Bake covered for 1 hour at 300F.
Carefully remove foil and bake for another 20 minutes at 375F.
Watch to make sure you do not burn the cheese.
Cool for ½ hour - serve with your favorite salad and cheesy garlic calabrese bread.

Rick Thorpe, MLA
Okanagan-Penticton

To-Die-For Veggie Lasagna

Rick Thorpe, MLA, Okanagan-Westside, British Columbia, Minister of Competition, Science and Enterprise

1 box lasagna noodles
1 cup diced broccoli
1 cup diced carrots
1 cup diced cauliflower
1 cup diced zucchini
1 cup diced celery
1 cup diced onions
1/2 cup diced red pepper
1/2 cup diced yellow pepper
1 cup sliced mushrooms
3 cloves crushed garlic
1/2 cup olive oil
1 large sprig basil (chopped)
1 large sprig fresh thyme
1 large sprig fresh rosemary
1 large spring fresh oregano (chopped)
1 large sprig fresh cilantro (chopped)
1 796 ml can chopped stewed tomatoes
1 398 ml can whole leaf spinach (drain liquid and chop)
1 700 ml jar Classico pasta sauce (my favourite: tomato and pesto)
2 cups grated sharp (old) cheddar cheese
2 cups grated mozzarella cheese
1 500 ml tub 2% cottage cheese

Over medium fire heat oil in large pot with lid. Add onion and garlic – fry for 2 minutes (stir often). Add all diced and sliced veggies. Stir, reduce heat and cover. Cook for 10 minutes, stirring occasionally.

Add spices, tomatoes, pasta sauce and chopped spinach. Bring to a boil – reducing heat. Cover and cook for another 10 minutes – stirring to prevent sticking or burning. Remove from heat and discard spice stalks from thyme and rosemary.

Assemble lasagna in a 13″ x 9″ x 2″ dish as follows. Ladle a little veggie sauce in the bottom of the dish first. Lay out noodles to cover dish bottom. Ladle sauce over noodles and cover with 1/2 the cheddar cheese. Repeat layer of noodles and sauce and cover with 1/2 the mozzarella cheese. Repeat layer of noodles and sauce and cover with the tub of cottage cheese. Repeat layer of noodles and sauce and cover with remaining cheddar cheese. Top layer of noodles and sauce and cover with remainder of the mozzarella cheese. Cover loosely with tin foil. (Lasagna may be frozen at this time – defrost before baking.) Bake covered for 1 hour at 300°F. Carefully remove foil and bake for 20 minutes at 375°F. Watch to make sure you do not burn the cheese. Cool for 1/2 hour – serve with your favourite salad and cheesy garlic calabrese bread. (Recipe on page 165.)

– (TESTER) MIKE LARGE, CHEF GUN BARREL GRILL RESTAURANT.

"THIS IS SO INCREDIBLE, WE INCLUDED IT ON OUR MENU AS ONE OF THE 'IRONMAN CANADA' CARBO LOAD DISHES."

– (TASTER) WENDY BOSMA, OWNER GUN BARREL GRILL RESTAURANT.

"I am an elected official; a mere reflection of those who voted for me."

P.01

NOV-16-1999 14:15 PETER ADAMS MP

HOUSE OF COMMONS
CHAMBRE DES COMMUNES
OTTAWA, CANADA
K1A 0A6

PETER ADAMS, M.P.
PETERBOROUGH

Fax ~~205~~ 250 - 493 - 7174

Attn Yasmin

This gives Yasmin full permission to use my recipe etc.

Peter Adams

OTTAWA
Room 158
Confederation Building
Ottawa, K1A 0A6
Tel: (613) 995-6411
Fax: (613) 996-9800

PETERBOROUGH
313 Water St.
Peterborough, Ont
K9J 7W7
Tel: (705) 745-2108
toll free 1-800-567-8554
Fax: (705) 741-4123

TOTAL P.01

ABC (Adams Broccoli Concoction)

Peter Adams, MP, Peterborough, Ontario

1 bunch broccoli, cut in small pieces, uncooked
1 cup raisins
1/4 cup diced red onion
10 strips or 1/2 pound bacon, fried and crumbled
3/4 to 1 cup sunflower seeds

Dressing

2 tablespoons sugar
1/3 cup mayonnaise
1 tablespoon vinegar (wine or cider)

Mix dressing and pour over above ingredients.

Make 4–5 hours ahead, but <u>not</u> overnight.

"EASY TO PREPARE AND VERY TASTY. WOULD BE AN EXCELLENT DISH FOR PICNICS AND POTLUCK MEALS."

– (TESTER) PATRICIA MATEJU, CHOIR MEMBER.

Notes:

"I usually double everything in anticipation of the great demand."

Minister
of Citizenship
and Immigration

Ministre
de la Citoyenneté
et de l'Immigration

Ottawa, Canada K1A 1L1

OCT. 20 2000

Ms. Yasmin John-Thorpe
150 Adamson Court
Penticton, BC V2A 7R8

Dear Ms. John-Thorpe:

Thank you for your letter of August 15, 2000, concerning your cookbook, "Taking the Heat: Canadian Politicians in the Kitchen".

As requested, I have enclosed copies of a few of my favourite easy recipes for inclusion in your book.

Best wishes for a successful publication.

Sincerely,

Elinor Caplan

Canada

Egg Soufflé Casserole

Elinor Caplan, MP, Thornhill, Ontario, Minister of Citizenship and Immigration

Make two days in advance.

8 eggs
4 cups milk
10 slices bread, buttered & cubed with crust off
2 pounds grated cheddar cheese
1 teaspoon dry mustard
2 tablespoons curry powder
2 teaspoons salt
1/4 teaspoon pepper

Lightly beat eggs and milk together. In an ungreased casserole alternate layers of cheese and bread. Stir seasonings into egg and milk mixture and pour over cheese and bread. Cover in fridge for 48 hours. Remove 2 hours before baking at 350°F for 40 minutes. Serves 8.

"ADVANCE PREPARATION MAKES THIS A VERY EASY DISH FOR THE BUSY EXECUTIVE. CHEESY AND RICH TASTING. CURRY ADDS STRONG FLAVOUR; USE LESS IF DESIRED."

– (TESTER) YASMIN JOHN-THORPE, WRITER AND COOKBOOK COMPILER.

Notes:

Bob Mills, MP
(Red Deer)

Ottawa
653-D Centre Block
Ottawa, Ontario
K1A 0A6
(613) 995-0590
FAX: (613) 995-6831
Internet: millsb@parl.gc.ca

Red Deer
4921-47th St.
Red Deer, Alberta T4N 1R4
(403) 347-7426
Fax: (403) 347-7423
1-800-667-0523
Internet: bmillsmp@telusplanet.net

October 14, 1999

Yasmin John-Thorpe,
150 Adamson Court,
Penticton, B.C.
V2A 7R8

Dear Yasmin:

Thank you for your recent e-mail regarding a cookbook you are compiling entitled Taking the Heat: Canadian Politicians in the Kitchen. I appreciate the time you have taken to write.

Please find attached 3 different recipes, which I hope you will find useful.

Also enclosed are 2 quotes that I would like to submit, as requested.

Lastly, you will find a photo that you also required, which I hope will suffice.

Again, thank you for writing and good luck with the book!

Best wishes.

Yours truly,

Bob Mills

Bob Mills, MP
Red Deer

Easy French Onion Soup

Bob Mills, MP, Red Deer, Alberta

8 cups beef broth
2 tablespoons olive oil
3 tablespoons butter
8-10 large yellow onions, sliced
1 large clove garlic, mashed
1 teaspoon fresh ground black pepper
1 1/2 tablespoons flour
1 cup dry red wine
6-8 medium slices toasted French bread
1 1/2 cups Gruyere cheese, shredded

Combine olive oil and butter in a heavy pot and heat. Add onions; sauté very slowly over low heat, stirring often until dark brown, about 30-40 minutes. Add garlic and pepper. Sprinkle in flour and stir. In a separate pan bring beef broth to a boil. Add to onion mixture and cook slowly for 10 minutes.

Pour soup into individual crocks and top with the sliced toast, cover with the shredded cheese and bake in a 400°F oven until cheese is bubbly, about 10 minutes.

This soup is wonderful with a crisp green salad and a glass of wine!

"DIFFERENT. A LITTLE THICKER THAN THE STANDARD SOUP. A PLEASANT TASTE."

– (TESTER) ALAN E. LONGWORTH, WRITER.

Notes:

Quoted from The Boston Globe *on 07/09/00: "Much of what they're saying sounds good, wonderful, in a perfect world," Bob Mills said. "But the UN has proven it can't respond to world issues." "I'm one who thinks the world is a better place for having Canada," he added.*

#20

PORRIDGE BREAD

2 cups boiling WATER
1 cup Rolled oats
2 tablespoons shortening
½ cup molasses
2 teaspoons salt
5–6 cups WATER
(Disolve 1 yeast in ½ cup water with 1 teaspoon of sugar and set aside)

Pour water over Rolled oats, Add shortening and cool. Add all ~~ingredients~~ ingredients & mix. Let rise. Pan & let rise again.
Bake 40–50 minutes at 350°

REVISED – PORRIDGE BREAD.
1½ lb. BREAD machine.

1¼ cups water
2 tablespoons shortening
2 tablespoons Powdered mil[k]
3 " " molasses
1 " " brown sugar
1½ teaspoon salt.
2¾ cups white flour
2/3 cup Rolled oats
1¾ teaspoons yeast
Set on "GRAIN" 4 hrs

Note:
This dates back at least 200 yrs in our family
Jim D.

JIM DEWOLFE
MLA - Pictou East
Province of Nova Scotia

Porridge Bread

Jim Dewolfe, MLA, Picton East, Nova Scotia

2 cups boiling water
1 cup rolled oats
2 tablespoons shortening
1/2 cup molasses
2 teaspoons salt
5–6 cups water

Notes:

Dissolve yeast in 1/2 cup water with 1 teaspoon of sugar and set aside.

Pour water over rolled oats, add shortening and cool. Add all ingredients and mix. Let rise. Pan and let rise again.

Bake 40–50 minutes at 350°F.

Revised Porridge Bread

(For 1 1/2 pound Bread Machine)

1 1/4 cups water
2 tablespoons shortening
2 tablespoons powdered milk
3 tablespoons molasses
1 tablespoon brown sugar
1 1/2 teaspoons salt
2 3/4 cups white flour
2/3 cup rolled oats
1 3/4 teaspoons yeast

Set on "Grain" 4 hours.

"Makes two loaves. You can taste the molasses. It is a bit heavy and a little like whole wheat. Hearty taste to it. If using the bread machine, bake for 3 1/2 hours."

– (Tester) Penny Smith, young-adult author.

"This dates back at least 200 years in our family."

JOHN R. O'TOOLE

Member of Provincial Parliament
Durham

Ontario

November 4, 1999

Ms. Yasmin John-Thorpe
150 Adamson Court
Penticton, British Columbia
V2A 7R8

Dear Ms. John-Thorpe:

Thank you for your email inviting me to submit a recipe for your new cookbook, entitled "Taking the Heat: Canadian Politicians in the Kitchen".

I am pleased to provide you with one of my favourite recipes for Chili Sauce.

Please do not hesitate to contact me if you have any further questions. My email address is: john_otoole@ontla.ola.org .

Best of success with the publication of your project!

Yours truly,

John R. O'Toole, MPP
Durham

Encl.

☐ Legislative Office: 250 Yonge St. • 35th Floor • Toronto • Ontario M5B 2N5 • Tel. (416) 325-6745 • Fax (416) 325-6255
☐ Constituency Office: 75 King St. E. • Bowmanville • Ontario L1C 1N4 • Tel. 1-800-661-2433 • (905) 697-1501 • Fax (905) 697-1506

Chili Sauce

John R. O'Toole, MPP, Durham, Ontario

6 quarts ripe tomatoes
4 cups chopped celery
4 cups chopped onions
1/4 cup pickling salt

Notes:

Let stand overnight. Next day drain off juice and add:

2 chopped green peppers
1 chopped sweet red pepper
2 cups white vinegar
2 tablespoons mustard seed
2 cups white sugar

Boil 1/2 hour. May need draining. Bottle.

"Easy to make. Would make a tasty sauce for grilled chicken."
– (Tester) Carmen Goncalves, health care worker.

"Test out on strangers first."

Prince Edward Island

Office of the Premier

95 Rochford Street
PO Box 2000
Charlottetown
Prince Edward Island
Canada C1A 7N8

Tel 902 368 4400
Fax 902 368 4416
http://www.gov.pe.ca/

Île-du-Prince-Édouard

Cabinet du Premier ministre

95, rue Rochford
C.P. 2000
Charlottetown
Île-du-Prince-Édouard
Canada C1A 7N8

Tél. 902 368 4400
Téléc. 902 368 4416
http://www.gov.pe.ca/

March 30, 2000

Ms. Yasmine John-Thorpe
150 Adamson Court
Penticton
BC V2A 7R8

Dear Ms. John-Thorpe:

I am happy to respond to your fax of March 23, 2000.

Besides my career as Premier of Prince Edward Island, my wife and I operate a bean farm and a bean processing plant (edible beans). The name of our company is "Island Bean", and I am pleased to provide you with a favorite family recipe for baked beans.

Please accept my best wishes for success in completion of "Taking the Heat: Canadian Politicians in the Kitchen."

Sincerely,

Pat Binns
Premier of Prince Edward Island

/nf

Enclosures

Island Baked Beans

Pat Binns, MLA, Murray River–Gaspereaux, Premier of Prince Edward Island

*1 1/2 cups Island Bean yellow eye beans**
1/2 small onion
1/3 cup molasses
1/4 cup brown sugar
1 teaspoon dry mustard
1 tablespoon ketchup (optional)
Bacon slices (optional)
1 teaspoon salt
1/2 teaspoon pepper

Notes:

Sort beans by hand. Rinse dry beans and soak overnight in cold water. Drain beans and cover with 6 cups of water. Use a heavy pot! Bring to a boil, reduce heat and parboil gently until beans are almost tender. Drain and rinse beans in cold water, but save about 4 cups of the cooking water. Put beans in a 2 L sized oven casserole. Mix all other ingredients with the 4 cups of cooking water; add to beans. Bake, covered, at 350°F until desired tenderness and consistency is reached. Add more water during baking if needed.

**A quick soak method can be used instead of an overnight soak.

"My husband and I thought they were great. The brown sugar adds just enough sweetness and the recipe makes just the right amount so leftovers are few."

– (Tester) Rose Hennessey, Prince Edward Island resident.

** Compiler's note: These beans are not available across Canada. Premier Binns explains that they are found only as far west as Ontario.*

Prince Edward Island
Legislative Assembly

Government Members' Office
PO Box 338
Charlottetown
Prince Edward Island
Canada C1A 7K7

Tel 902 368 4360
Fax 902 368 4377
www.gov.pe.ca/

Île-du-Prince-Édouard
Assemblée législative

Bureau des députés provinciaux
C.P. 338
Charlottetown
Île-du-Prince-Édouard
Canada C1A 7K7

Tél. : 902 368 4360
Téléc. : 902 368 4377
www.gov.pe.ca/

March 30, 2001

Ms. Yasmine John-Thorpe
150 Adamson Court
Penticton, BC V2A 7R8

Dear Ms. John-Thorpe:

Thank you for requesting my favourite recipe to include in your cookbook.

This recipe, Barbeque Sauce, is a great favourite with our family. It is a little sweet and a little tart and great on just about any kind of meat for barbequing. I certainly hope all your readers will enjoy it.

I truly wish you the very best of luck with your cookbook, "Taking the Heat: Canadian Politicians in the Kitchen."

Sincerely,

Norman MacPhee, MLA
District 17
Crapaud - Hazel Grove

aah
Enclosure

Barbecue Sauce

Norman MacPhee, MLA, Crapaud-Hazel Grove, Prince Edward Island

This particular recipe is for barbecue spareribs, but it is also very good on pork chops, steak, ground beef, etc.

Place spareribs in cooking dish, dice one onion and sprinkle over spareribs and then place in 400°F preheated oven.

Meanwhile, in a saucepan, mix the following:

1 cup ketchup
1/4 cup vinegar
1 teaspoon prepared mustard
1 cup water
2 tablespoons brown sugar
2 teaspoons salt
Pepper to taste

Bring mixture to a boil, pour over spareribs, reduce oven temperature to 350°F and bake for 2 hours.

"STRAIGHTFORWARD AND EASY TO PREPARE."

– (TESTER) YASMIN JOHN-THORPE, WRITER AND COOKBOOK COMPILER.

Notes:

"This recipe, Barbecue Sauce, is a great favourite with our family. It is a little sweet and a little tart and great on just about any kind of meat for barbecuing."

CABINET DU LIEUTENANT-GOUVERNEUR
QUÉBEC

Je pense très souvent à tous ces jeunes parents qui, après le travail, se hâtent de revenir à la maison pour retrouver les leurs et profiter des joies de la famille enfin réunie. Ils sont conscients de la nécessité d'avoir une alimentation équilibrée, mais ils n'ont pas toujours le temps, par exemple, d'étuver les tomates, de tailler les légumes, de préparer un recette qui nécessite plusieurs étapes.

Alors, pour tous ceux et celles qui font la cuisine de l'an 2000, j'ai simplifié au maximum ce plat.

Le Gaspacho du Riche

Ingrédients

Déposer dans un mélangeur et actionner quelques secondes, jusqu'à la consistance voulue :

- 1 boîte de tomates de 16 onces
- 1 piment vert
- ½ concombre
- 6 gousses d'ail
- 2 tasses de consommé
- ⅓ tasse de mayonnaise
- 2 c. à table de vinaigre
- Sel, poivre
- ¼ tasse de chapelure
- ¼ tasse d'amandes en poudre

Préparation

Réfrigérer. Au moment de servir, ajouter ¼ tasse de crème 35 %. Couper les légumes suivants et les déposer dans de petits bols, ils serviront de garniture : concombres, échalotes, tomates et piments. On peut également ajouter quelques cubes de pain sec.

Lise Thibault
Lieutenant-gouverneur du Québec

Le Gaspacho du Riche

Lise Thibault, Lieutenant-gouverneur du Québec

Déposer dans un mélangeur et actionner quelques secondes, jusqu'à la consistance voulue:
1 boîte de tomates de 16 onces
1 piment vert
1/2 concombre
6 gousses d'ail
2 tasses de consummé
1/3 tasse de mayonnaise
2 c. à table de vinaigre
Sel, poivre
1/4 tasse de chapelure
1/4 tasse d'amandes en poudre

Préparation:

Réfrigérer. Au moment de servir, ajouter 1/4 tasse de crème 35%. Couper les légumes suivants et les déposer dans de petits bols, ils serviront de garniture: concombres, échalotes, tomates et piments. On peut également ajouter quelques cubes de pain sec.

UN PLAT TRES NOURISSANT, AVEC UN AVANT GÔUT DU PRINTEMPS. FACILE À APPRÊTER. MERCI BEAUCOUP POUR LA RECETTE.

– (TESTER) NATHALIE LEWIS, DÈCORATRICE D'INTERIEUR ET ARTISANE.

Notes:

"Je pense très souvent à tous ces jeunes parents qui, après le travail, se hâtent de revenir à la maison pour retrouver les leurs et profiter des joies de la famille enfin réunie. Ils sont conscients de la nécessité d'avoir une alimentation équilibrée, mais ils n'ont pas toujours le temps, par exemple, d'étuver les tomates, de tailler les légumes, de préparer un recette qui nécessite plusieurs étapes. Alors, pour tous ceux et celles qui font la cuisine de l'an 2000, j'ai simplifié au maximum ce plat."

PREMIER OF SASKATCHEWAN

LEGISLATIVE BUILDING
REGINA CANADA S4S 0B3

April 16, 2001

2039/2001

Yasmin John-Thorpe
Casa Bella Vista
4011 Finnerty Road
PENTICTON BC V2A 8W2

Dear Ms. John-Thorpe:

Thank you for your recent letter regarding your cookbook *Taking the Heat: Canadian Politicians in the Kitchen*. I am pleased to provide you with the requested information.

I have attached a copy of one of my favourite recipes. You may wish to include this quote with the recipe:

"A hungry man is not a free man."
Adlai E. Stevenson

With respect to your request for a photograph, as I do not have an official photo at this time you may wish to use the photograph that is on the Saskatchewan government website:

www.gov.sk.ca/govinfo/premier/

Again, thank you for writing, and best wishes for your cookbook.

Yours sincerely,

Lorne Calvert
Premier

Enclosure

www.gov.sk.ca

pcu-regina

Premier Calvert's Favourite German Pancakes

Lorne Calvert, MLA, Saskatoon Riversdale, Premier of Saskatchewan

4 eggs
1 tablespoon sugar
1/2 teaspoon salt
2/3 cup flour
2/3 cup milk
2 tablespoons soft butter

Notes:

Heat oven to 400°F. Butter well two 9" cake pans. Put eggs into blender and process on STIR until they are light yellow in colour. Add remaining ingredients and MIX until smooth.

Pour into pans and bake for 20 minutes, then reduce heat to 350°F and bake 10 minutes.

Slide onto hot plate and serve with lemon slices, powdered sugar and butter. Syrup, Jello or honey may also be used.

Serves 2-3; however, this recipe can easily be doubled.

The Premier and his family prefer to top the pancakes with mixed fruit slices and whipped cream, and serve with bacon and sausages. Great to serve to guests for a special brunch!

"Very easy to prepare. I liked the texture."
– (Tester) Patricia Mateju, choir member.

"A hungry man is not a free man."

#35

Eric Cline, MLA

Saskatoon Mount Royal
#3 - 2102 - 22nd Street West
Saskatoon, SK S7M 0V3
Phone: (306) 384-7200
Fax: (306) 384-4280

203 Legislative Building
Regina, SK S4S 0B3
Phone: (306) 787-0893 (collect)

2 February 2000

Yasmin John-Thorpe
150 Adamson Court
Penticton, BC
V2A 7R8

Dear Ms. John-Thorpe,

Thank you for inviting me to participate in your cookbook for the new millennium, which portrays elected members doing a simple, ordinary everyday task. I am enclosing a pancake recipe, my biography, picture and a quote. I hope that you can use this in your cookbook.

Best wishes to you and your cookbook project.

Sincerely,

Eric Cline, MLA

EC/der

Enclosure

Pancakes - Basic Recipe

Eric Cline, MLA, Saskatoon Mount Royal, Saskatchewan, Minister of Finance

1 egg
1 3/4 cups milk
3 tablespoons white sugar
1 1/2 cups flour
3 teaspoons baking powder
1/2 teaspoon salt
3 teaspoons soft margarine or shortening
1/4 teaspoon vanilla

Notes:

Beat egg till light. Add milk and sugar. Add sifted dry ingredients and beat only enough to make a smooth batter. Stir in softened margarine and vanilla.

Heat griddle, brush lightly with oil; drop batter by tablespoons or pour onto griddle. Cook until pancakes are brown and filled with bubbles. Turn and cook on other side. Do not turn more than once.

Serve hot with your favourite toppings.

This recipe makes 12 good-sized pancakes.

Banana Pancakes

To the above, add one mashed banana, and you have very nice banana pancakes.

"EASY. MAKE SURE BANANAS ARE VERY RIPE IF YOU LIKE A STRONGER BANANA FLAVOUR."

– (TASTER) PATRICIA MATEJU, CHOIR MEMBER.

"To those who say they don't like politicians, I would ask: 'How can you have a democracy without elected people, i.e. politicians?' To those who ask: 'How good are our politicians?' I would say 'about as good as the people who elect them and take the time to pay attention to political affairs.' The only valid reason to enter political life is public service. I'm proud to be a politician and to have the opportunity to serve my friends and neighbours in the Legislature."

Glenn Hagel, M.L.A.
MOOSE JAW NORTH

640 Main St. N., Moose Jaw, Saskatchewan S6H 3K4 **Phone: (306) 694-1001** Fax: (306) 691-0486 Regina: (306) 787-1886
moose.jaw.mlas@sk.sympatico.ca

March 31, 2000

Ms. Jasmin John-Thorpe
150 Adamson Court
PENTICTION BC V2A 7R8

Dear Ms. ~~John-Thorpe~~ Jasmin:

I am writing in response to your recent letter faxed here March 22, 2000, requesting a recipe for your cookbook titled "TAKING THE HEAT: Canadian Politicians in the Kitchen".

Here is the recipe I am enclosing:

#37 **PANCAKES THAT STICK TO THE ROOF OF YOUR HOUSE**
(They're that light and fluffy!)

This recipe is guaranteed to make a hero out of any dad who's conducting his monthly Sunday brunch production.

2 Cups sifted all-purpose flour
4 Tablespoons baking power
4 Tablespoons sugar
1 Teaspoon salt
2 Beaten eggs
2 Cups milk
3 Tablespoons salad oil

METHOD: Combine, eggs, milk and salad oil. Sift together dry ingredients; add to liquid ingredients, stirring just till moistened. Bake on hot griddle. Sprinkle water on griddle. If drops dance, heat is perfect and you're on your way. Flip pancakes-enough for 4-6 hungry munchkins of any age or size.

Ms. John-Thorpe
March 28,2000
Page 2

Freeze leftover pancakes, to be reheated in your toaster on a morning when you've slept in. Serve with eggs, sausage or bacon or whatever you can persuade the kids to make while your producing this gourmet delight. Top with butter and your favorite syrup. Eat quickly, before these feather pancakes float off the plate, right up to your ceiling. Enjoy!

My quote to go with this recipe is **"A comfortable tummy sets the stage for a curious mind."**

With warm personal regards, I wish you success with your cookbook and have enclosed with this fantastic recipe my photo.

Sincerely,

Glenn Hagel

Glenn Hagel, MLA
Moose Jaw North

/cm

Pancakes (That stick to the roof of your house – they're that light and fluffy!)

Glenn Hagel, MLA, Moose Jaw North, Saskatchewan, Minister of Post-Secondary Education and Skills Training

This recipe is guaranteed to make a hero out of any dad who's conducting his monthly Sunday brunch production.

2 cups sifted all-purpose flour
4 tablespoons baking powder
4 tablespoons sugar
1 teaspoon salt
2 eggs, beaten
2 cups milk
3 tablespoons salad oil

Combine eggs, milk and salad oil. Sift together dry ingredients; add to liquid ingredients, stirring just till moistened. Bake on hot griddle. Sprinkle water on griddle first. If drops dance, heat is perfect and you're on your way. Flip pancakes. Enough for 4-6 hungry munchkins of any age or size.

Freeze leftover pancakes, to be reheated in your toaster on a morning when you've slept in. Serve with eggs, sausage or bacon or whatever you can persuade the kids to make while you're producing this gourmet delight. Top with butter and syrup. Eat quickly, before these feather pancakes float off the plate, right up to your ceiling. Enjoy!

"Easy to prepare."

– (Tester) Yasmin John-Thorpe, writer and cookbook compiler.

"These are great, Yas. Taste better than Momma's."

– (Taster) Donovan Abbott (age 5)

Notes:

"A comfortable tummy sets the stage for a curious mind."

Blender Hollandaise Sauce With Asparagus

Elinor Caplan, MP, Thornhill, Ontario, Minister of Citizenship and Immigration

4 egg yolks
1 3/4 tablespoons lemon juice
1/4 teaspoon salt
Dash Tabasco
2 teaspoons dry mustard
1/4 pound butter
1 pound asparagus

Put first 5 ingredients in blender and buzz for 1 minute. Just before serving, heat butter almost to boiling. Pour in steady stream into blender mixture, blend until smooth and creamy. Cook asparagus and top with hollandaise.

"Easy to make. An excellent, smooth sauce. I used the juice of one whole lemon, a lot more than was called for, as I enjoy the lemony taste."

– (Tester) Maureen McDonald, sports enthusiast and adventure traveller.

Lazy Perogies

Doreen E. Hamilton, MLA, Regina Wascana Plains, Saskatchewan

12 lasagna noodles
2 cups creamed cottage cheese
1 egg
1/4 teaspoon onion salt
1/4 teaspoon pepper
1/4 cup butter
1 cup shredded cheddar cheese
2 cups mashed potatoes
1 large onion, chopped

Cook noodles. Drain and rinse. Place 4 noodles in 9″x13″ baking dish as first layer.

Mix cottage cheese, egg, onion, salt and pepper, and spoon evenly over noodles. Place another layer of noodles on top. Mix cheddar cheese with seasoned mashed potatoes. Spoon over noodle layer. Now cover with remaining noodles. Sauté onions in butter and spoon over top. Bake at 350°F for 30-45 minutes. Serve with sour cream.

"Easy and satisfying dish. Would be good with the addition of ham or bacon."

– (Tester) Carolee Finch, office manager/ bookkeeper and outdoors enthusiast.

Cheese Garlic Bread

Rick Thorpe, MLA, Okanagan-Westside, British Columbia, Minister of Competition, Science and Enterprise

1 fresh calabrese bread
1/2 cup butter
4 cloves crushed garlic
Parmesan cheese
1 large sprig chopped parsley

Melt butter in saucepan, adding garlic and parsley. Cook about 2 minutes – remove from heat. Slice bread and slightly overlap on large piece of tin foil. Drizzle butter mixture over bread making sure most slices are moist with butter. Sprinkle cheese over bread, wrap in foil and bake for 15 minutes at 375°F. Enjoy!

"THIS IS THE EASIEST, TASTIEST GARLIC BREAD EVER! A GOOD ADDITION TO VEGGIE LASAGNA (SEE PAGE 141) OR ANY PASTA DISH."

– (TESTER) YASMIN JOHN-THORPE, WRITER AND COOKBOOK COMPILER.

Jade Cheese Salad

Sue Edelman, MLA, Riverdale South, Yukon, Minister of Tourism

1 package green Jello (small)
1 cup boiling water
1 cup very cold water
1 teaspoon vinegar
Pinch of salt and pepper
1 cup cottage cheese
1 cup Miracle Whip

Mix first 5 ingredients and refrigerate till almost set. Mix jelly mixture until frothy and then add cottage cheese and Miracle Whip. Serve.

"This is the perfect low-calorie, light summer salad. It looks beautiful in a nice bowl when you bring it to summer barbecues!" – Sue Edelman

"VERY SIMPLE AND REFRESHING SALAD. I USED LOW FAT MAYONNAISE AND COTTAGE CHEESE."

– (TESTER) JUDY NICHOLAS, BIKER, HIKER AND YOGA INSTRUCTOR.

Muttar Chawal (Rice and Peas)

Sindi Hawkins, MLA, Okanagan–Mission, British Columbia, Minister Responsible for Health Planning

2 cups basmati (Indian long grain) rice
1 large onion, finely sliced
4 cardamom seeds, crushed
2 cinnamon sticks
2 1/2 cups boiling water
1 cup chopped fresh coriander sprigs
3 tablespoons oil
6 cloves
2 teaspoons salt
2 bay leaves
2 cups frozen peas

Rinse rice several times in cold water and drain. Let rice soak in cold, clear water for at least 20 minutes before cooking. Drain thoroughly. Heat oil in medium pot. Lightly brown onion, add cloves, cardamom seeds, bay leaves, cinnamon sticks, peas and salt. Cook until peas are well heated. Add rice and heat thoroughly, before adding boiling water. Bring mixture to a boil. Lower heat, cover and cook for 20–25 minutes. Do not lift the lid to peek until the rice is cooked. Garnish with fresh coriander sprigs. Accompanies Chicken Curry with Yogurt, page 51.

Inniskillin

Inniskillin Wines Inc.
Niagara Parkway & Line 3
R.R. 1, Niagara-on-the-Lake
Ontario, Canada L0S 1J0
Telephone: (905) 468-2187
Telefax: (905) 468-5355
Toll Free: 1-888-466-4754
e-mail: inniskil@inniskillin.com

Inniskillin Okanagan Vineyards Inc.
Road II, R.R. #1 S24, C5
Oliver, British Columbia
Canada V0H 1T0
Telephone: (250) 498-6663
Telefax: (250) 498-4566
Toll Free: 1-800-498-6211

Web Sites:
http://www.inniskillin.com
http://www.icewine.com

ICEWINE:

Canada's Niagara Peninsula in Ontario and the Okanagan Valley in British Columbia are considered cool climate viticulture regions, as are Burgundy, Germany, Oregon and New Zealand. Wines from cooler climates are characteristically higher in acids and highly aromatic.

The most famous of all cool climate wines is of course Icewine. The grapes are left on the vine well into December and January. The ripe berries are dehydrated through the constant freezing and thawing during these winter conditions. The remarkable process concentrates the sugars, acids and extracts in the berries thereby intensifying the flavours and giving Icewine its immense complexity.

The grapes are painstakingly picked by hand in their naturally frozen state, ideally at temperature of −10 to −13 degrees C, sometimes forcing the pickers out in the middle of the night. The frozen grapes are pressed in the extreme cold. Much of the water in the juice remains frozen as ice crystals during the pressing and only a few drops of sweet concentrated juice are salvaged. The juice is then fermented very slowly for several mothers and stops naturally at approximately 10-12 percent alcohol.

Icewine tastes intensely sweet and flavourful in the initial mouth sensation. The balance is achieved by the acidity, which creates a clean, dry finish to the taste. The nose is reminiscent of lychee nuts and the wine tastes of tropical fruits with overtones of peach nectar and mango. Primarily, the quality of Icewine is determined by how low the temperature drops at the time of harvest, resulting in the high extract, fullness and concentration of aroma in the final product. Another major characteristic of Icewine is its naturally high acidity, which is a direct function of cool climate viticulture regions. It is the acidity, which distinguishes Icewine from most other dessert wines. This ideal equilibrium along with the intensity of sugar created by natural freezing process, make Icewine such a unique and truly great wine.

Donald J. P. Ziraldo
Co-founder & President

Inniskillin Anniversary 1975 25 2000

Icewine

Canada's Niagara Peninsula in Ontario and the Okanagan Valley in British Columbia are considered cool climate viticulture regions, as are Burgundy, Germany, Oregon and New Zealand. Wines from cooler climates are characteristically higher in acids and highly aromatic.

The most famous of all cool climate wines is of course Icewine. The grapes are left on the vine well into December and January. The ripe berries are dehydrated through the constant freezing and thawing during these winter conditions. The remarkable process concentrates the sugars, acids and extracts in the berries, thereby intensifying the flavours and giving Icewine its immense complexity.

The grapes are painstakingly picked by hand in their naturally frozen state, ideally at temperatures of -10° to -13°C, sometimes forcing the pickers out in the middle of the night. The frozen grapes are pressed in the extreme cold. Much of the water in the juice remains frozen as ice crystals during the pressing and only a few drops of sweet concentrated juice are salvaged. The juice is then fermented very slowly for several months and stops naturally at approximately 10-12 percent alcohol.

Icewine tastes intensely sweet and flavourful in the initial mouth sensation. The balance is achieved by the acidity, which creates a clean, dry finish to the taste. The nose is reminiscent of lychee nuts and the wine tastes of tropical fruits with overtones of peach nectar and mango. Primarily, the quality of Icewine is determined by how low the temperature drops at the time of harvest, resulting in the high extract, fullness and concentration of aroma in the final product. Another major characteristic of Icewine is its naturally high acidity, which is a direct function of cool climate viticulture regions. It is the acidity which distinguishes Icewine from most other dessert wines. This ideal equilibrium, along with the intensity of sugar created by natural freezing process, make Icewine such a unique and truly great wine.

Donald J. P. Ziraldo, President and Co-founder,
Inniskillin Wines Inc., Niagara-on-the-Lake, Ontario,
Inniskillin Okanagan Vineyards Inc., Oliver, British Columbia
Author of "Anatomy of a Winery" and "Anatomy of a Winery – Millennium Edition"

SUMAC RIDGE
ESTATE WINERY

VINTER'S QUALITY ALLIANCE

WHAT IS VQA?

The Vintner's Quality Alliance (VQA) is both a provincial and national wine standard for quality control from the vineyard to the glass. It is modeled after an Old World system very much like the Appellation Controllée of France (AOC), DOC of Italy and QMP of Germany. It is the consumer's only assurance of quality and excellence made within Canada.

HOW DID VQA COME ABOUT IN BRITISH COLUMBIA?

VQA is the end result of more than twelve years of effort by a technical committee comprised of winemakers and grape growers in the Okanagan Valley working together to develop credible wine standards that would stand up to international scrutiny. The Canada/US Free Trade Agreement signed in 1988 accelerated the process and until that time the British Columbia industry was contemplating calling it's yet to be implemented standards either Appellation British Columbia (ABC) or British Columbia Appellation (BCA).

At the same time Ontario vintners had developed very similar styles in their region and had registered the trademark VQA. It made perfect sense for us to have only one standard that would recognize quality for Canadian wines and so after dialogue with Donald Ziraldo in Ontario, the leading proponent of the VQA standard in that region, we came to agreement that we would adopt the same identification in British Columbia and work toward harmonization of the regions and British Columbia launched VQA on December 4, 1990.

THE VQA LOGO

Identification of VQA or the medallion/logo represents a commitment to quality with a guarantee that the wine expresses the highest aspiration of the vintner's art.

A wine bearing the VQA medallion is the consumer's only assurance of quality in British Columbia wines and ensures the consumer that:

- The bottle of wine is made from 100% British Columbia grown grapes.
- The wine has been made to VQA standards set and monitored by the British Columbia Wine Institute (BCWI) who's members include wineries of all sizes as well as grape growers (the standards apply to a minimum quality for grapes as well as wine).
- The wine has been approved as a result of blind tastings by an expert tasting panel.

THE VQA REGULATIONS

For a wine to bear a varietal name (i.e. the name of the grape) it must contain a minimum of 85% of the named grape variety as well as meet the expectation of the taste of the varietal characteristic associated with the variety.

Where the vintage is displayed, at least 95% of the grapes used must have been grown in the year indicated.

If there is a geographical indicator (example: "Okanagan Valley") the wine must contain a minimum 95% of grapes grown in that geographic area with the balance of grapes used coming from the province of British Columbia.

❋❋❋❋❋❋❋❋❋

Now with 10 years of VQA Standards in place and the marketing and recognition of the logo we are very confident that we have consumer acceptance that is well established and continues to grow. It is my personal opinion that the adoption of the VQA Standards for all Canadian Wines is probably the single most important factor in the acceptance and image of quality in the Canadian wine industry and has significantly changed attitudes and opened new marketing opportunities both nationally and internationally.

Good luck, good cooking and bon appetite.

Cheers!!

President, Sumac Ridge Estate Wine Group
Founding Chairman, British Columbia Wine Institute
Founding Chairman, VQA Canada

Vintner's Quality Alliance

The Vintner's Quality Alliance (VQA) is both a provincial and national wine standard for quality control from the vineyard to the glass. It is modelled after an Old World system very much like the Appellation Controllée of France (AOC), DOC of Italy and QMP of Germany. It is the consumer's only assurance of quality and excellence made within Canada.

VQA is the end result of more than twelve years of effort by a technical committee comprised of winemakers and grape growers in the Okanagan Valley working together to develop credible wine standards that would stand up to international scrutiny. The Canada/US Free Trade Agreement signed in 1988 accelerated the process and until that time the British Columbia industry was contemplating calling its yet to be implemented standards either Appellation British Columbia (ABC) or British Columbia Appellation (BCA).

Identification of VQA or the medallion/logo represents a commitment to quality with a guarantee that the wine expresses the highest aspiration of the vintner's art.

A wine bearing the VQA medallion is the consumer's only assurance of quality in British Columbia wines.

Now with 10 years of VQA Standards in place and the marketing and recognition of the logo we are very confident that we have consumer acceptance that is well established and continues to grow. It is my personal opinion that the adoption of the VQA Standards for all Canadian Wines is probably the single most important factor in the acceptance and image of quality in the Canadian wine industry and has significantly changed attitudes and opened new marketing opportunities both nationally and internationally.

Good luck, good cooking and bon appetite.
Cheers!!!

Harry McWatters
President, Sumac Ridge Estate Wine Group
Founding Chairman, British Columbia Wine Institute
Founding Chairman, VQA Canada

BRITISH COLUMBIA

October 28, 1999

Ms. Y. Thorpe
150 Adamson Court
Penticton, BC V2A 7R8

Dear Mrs. Thorpe;

Thank you for your letter of October 23, 1999. You are writing to clarify your involvement in a project on which you will be working in the coming months. You are a writer and presently collecting recipes from elected official from across Canada for a cookbook which is part of your contribution to the city of Penticton's millenium projects. You are the president of the company which will register the cookbook, your husband is the secretary/treasurer and your children are directors. Your husband, Rick Thorpe is the MLA for Okanagan-Penticton. Your request my opinion as to whether I see this project as a conflict of interest.

There is nothing in the facts placed before me which appears to constitute either a conflict or an apparent conflict of interest.

As Conflict of Interest Commissioner, I am of the opinion that it is perfectly proper for you to proceed. As the former charter president of the British Columbia Branch of the International Wine and Food Society, I wish you every success with this interesting project: if I say I believe it will form a valuable contribution to the culinary standards of Penticton, I hope that you will not interpret that as some form of hidden criticism of existing standards.

Yours sincerely,

H.A.D. Oliver
Commissioner

Office of the Conflict of Interest Commissioner

The Honourable H. A. D. Oliver, Q.C.
Commissioner

Mailing Address:
101 - 431 Menzies Street
Victoria BC V8V 1X4

Telephone: (250) 356-9283
Facsimile: (250) 356-6580

PENTICTON 2000 CELEBRATION

December 14, 2000

Mr. and Mrs. Rick and Yasmin Thorpe
Tobago International
150 Adamson Court
Penticton, BC V2A 7R8

Dear Mr. and Mrs. Thorpe,

On behalf of the Celebration 2000 Committee, I would like to thank you for registering your millennium project: *National Cookbook featuring Canadian Politicians.* Hundreds of Penticton area residents and organizations marked the millennium with a project or reunion, and our committee appreciates your special efforts and contribution to the community.

Yours very truly,
CELEBRATION 2000 COMMITTEE

Ken Jaggard

K. Jaggard
Chair

(0550.20 – 2000 Cel. 2000 – Merge Letter to Registrants)

c/o CITY OF PENTICTON, 171 MAIN STREET, PENTICTON, B.C. V2A 5A9 • PHONE (250) 490-2400 • FAX (250) 490-2402
www4.vip.net/c2kpenticton

Regrets...

Prime Minister Jean Chretien

Ms. Joanne Flemming responded in a telephone conversation that my request for a recipe from the Prime Minister is denied.

Rideau Hall

"On behalf of Her Excellency the Right Honourable Adrienne Clarkson, I am replying to your letter in which you request a recipe from the Governor General. I am sorry for the delay in this reply, but the high volume of correspondence which Rideau Hall received since the Governor General's appointment has made it difficult to answer letters as quickly as we wish. I regret to advise you that due to the large number of similar requests received, the policy has been adopted of not providing recipes. While this response must be disappointing to you, I am sure you understand that it would be most difficult for this office to adequately meet the demand."

Lieutenant Governor of Manitoba

"His Honour the Honourable Peter M. Liba, C.M., O.M., has asked me to acknowledge and thank you for your recent letter requesting a favourite recipe for publication in your cookbook 'Taking the Heat: Canadian Politicians in the Kitchen'. The Lieutenant Governor was most interested to learn of your project and was pleased to note that the proceeds are being donated to a very worthy cause. However, as a matter of policy, the Office of the Lieutenant Governor does not participate in fund-raising ventures and His Honour regrets that it is therefore not possible for him to accede to your request. His Honour has asked me to convey his best wishes for success in achieving your goals."

Premier Lucien Bouchard

"On behalf of Premier Lucien Bouchard, I wish to acknowledge receipt of your e-mail dated last October 4. I regret to inform you that, for the time being, we have decided not to take advantage of your offer."

Lieutenant Governor of Saskatchewan

"On behalf of the Lieutenant Governor of Saskatchewan, I wish to acknowledge and thank you for your recent letter. Her Honour was interested in reading of your venture to publish a cookbook titled 'Taking the Heat: Canadian Politicians in the Kitchen'. However, as Lieutenant Governor, Her Honour in unable to become involved in matters of this kind as set forth by the mandate of the office. Her Honour would like to thank you for your invitation to submit a favourite recipe and wish you every success in the exciting project."

Lieutenant Governor of Alberta

"Thank you for your letter inviting Her Honour, the Lieutenant Governor, The Honourable Lois E. Hole, C.M. to submit a favourite recipe for a cookbook you are compiling. We regret to advise the Lieutenant Governor will not be able to meet your deadline for submission. Her Honour wishes you success with your publishing venture."

Todd Hardy, MLA Yukon

"Sorry, I really do not know how to cook and would probably eat cereals, salads and rice potatoes if my family members were not such great cooks, especially my wife who also happens to be a politician. Actually I did prepare one dish for my daughter's birthday. Maybe I could consider this as it was a success though my family would know how sporadic I cook and would consider me a sham. One dish does not constitute a cook."

Kevin Deveaux, MLA Nova Scotia

"Thank you for your e-mail. I enjoy cooking and would love to send a recipe, but I need a little more information. Is the cookbook intended to raise money for a particular cause? If so, which one? Do we have a chance to view the layout of our page once it is finalized? Is there a publisher for the book?" (Compiler's note: After numerous messages to the MLA, I received no recipes.)

Laurie Blakeman, MLA, Edmonton-Centre

"Sorry I can't help you with this project – I don't cook (neither did my mother, perhaps it's genetic!)... but I do make excellent reservations."

Notes

Notes

TAKING The HEAT

Canadian Politicians in the Kitchen

Order Form

All sale proceeds (after net costs) will be donated to food banks

Name: ______________________ **Phone:** ____________

Address: ______________________ **Email:** ____________

City: ____________ **Prov.:** ______ **Postal Code:** ________

Shipping Rates

1 book	*$2.50*
2 books	*$2.75*
3 books	*$3.00*
4 books	*$3.50*
5 books	*$4.50*
6 books	*$4.75*
7 books	*$5.00*
8 books	*$5.50*
9 books	*$5.75*
10 books	*$6.50*
25 books	*$10.00*

1-9 Copies ***$15.95*** *ea.* ____ *copies @$15.95 =* ________

10 Copies ***$10.00*** *ea.* ____ *sets of 10 @$100.00 =* ________

25 Copies ***$9.50*** *ea.* ____ *sets of 25 @$237.50 =* ________

Shipping (see table at left): ________

Sub Total: ________

7% GST: ________

TOTAL ENCLOSED: ________

Send Money Order payable to:

Tobago International Inc.
Casa Bella Vista
4011 Finnerty Road
Penticton, British Columbia V2A 8W2
casabellavista@home.com

- -

TAKING The HEAT

Canadian Politicians in the Kitchen

Order Form

All sale proceeds (after net costs) will be donated to food banks

Name: ______________________ **Phone:** ____________

Address: ______________________ **Email:** ____________

City: ____________ **Prov.:** ______ **Postal Code:** ________

Shipping Rates

1 book	*$2.50*
2 books	*$2.75*
3 books	*$3.00*
4 books	*$3.50*
5 books	*$4.50*
6 books	*$4.75*
7 books	*$5.00*
8 books	*$5.50*
9 books	*$5.75*
10 books	*$6.50*
25 books	*$10.00*

1-9 Copies ***$15.95*** *ea.* ____ *copies @$15.95 =* ________

10 Copies ***$10.00*** *ea.* ____ *sets of 10 @$100.00 =* ________

25 Copies ***$9.50*** *ea.* ____ *sets of 25 @$237.50 =* ________

Shipping (see table at left): ________

Sub Total: ________

7% GST: ________

TOTAL ENCLOSED: ________

Send Money Order payable to:

Tobago International Inc.
Casa Bella Vista
4011 Finnerty Road
Penticton, British Columbia V2A 8W2
casabellavista@home.com